It's another great book from CGP...

This book is for anyone doing **GCSE OCR B Religious Studies: Ethics 1 & 2**.

It covers all the important information and issues in a **clear** and **balanced** way, with plenty of advice for writing **top-notch answers** in the exam. There's even a section to help you score full marks for your **spelling**, **punctuation** and **grammar**.

What's more, we've included a **free** Online Edition of the whole book, so you can revise on a computer or tablet — wherever you are.

How to get your free Online Edition

Just go to **cgpbooks.co.uk/extras** and enter this code...

4095 2940 2544 1803

By the way, this code only works for one person. If somebody else has used this book before you, they might have already claimed the Online Edition.

CGP — still the best! ☺

Our sole aim here at CGP is to produce the highest quality books — carefully written, immaculately presented and dangerously close to being funny.

Then we work our socks off to get them out to you — at the cheapest possible prices.

Contents

Ethics 1.1 — Religion and Human Relationships

- Roles of Men and Women 1
- Marriage in Christianity 2
- Marriage in Judaism 3
- Marriage in Islam 4
- Divorce 5
- Sexual Relationships 6
- Contraception 7
- Practice Questions 8

Ethics 1.2 — Religion and Medical Ethics

- Abortion 9
- Abortion: Judaism and Islam 10
- Fertility Treatment 11
- Euthanasia and Suicide 12
- Using Animals in Medical Research 14
- Practice Questions 15

Ethics 1.3 — Religion, Poverty and Wealth

- Wealth, Poverty and Disease 16
- Money and Charity: Christianity 17
- Money and Charity: Judaism 18
- Money and Charity: Islam 19
- Moral and Immoral Occupations 20
- Practice Questions 21

Ethics 2.1 — Religion, Peace and Justice

- Attitudes to War: Christianity 22
- Attitudes to War: Judaism 23
- Attitudes to War: Islam 24
- Law and Justice 25
- Punishment 26
- Social Injustice 27
- Practice Questions 28

Ethics 2.2 — Religion and Equality

Prejudice and Equality 29
Attitudes to Equality: Christianity 30
Attitudes to Equality: Islam 32
Attitudes to Equality: Judaism 33
Attitudes to Other Religions 34
Forgiveness and Reconciliation 36
Practice Questions 37

Ethics 2.3 — Religion and the Media

The Influence of the Media 38
Christianity in the Media 39
Judaism and Islam in the Media 40
Religion in Books and Films 41
Censorship and Freedom of Speech 42
Practice Questions 43

Do Well in Your Exam 44

Spelling, Punctuation and Grammar 46

Glossary 50

Index 52

Guide to Symbols

This book covers both Ethics Units in the context of **Christianity**, **Islam** and **Judaism**. The clouds in the corners of the pages tell you whether the page covers:

 the **Christian** view...

 ...the **Muslim** view...

 ...the **Jewish** view...

 ...or general views that **everyone** needs to learn.

Bible / Qur'an References

References from the Bible always go in the order: ***Book Chapter:Verse(s)***. So whenever you see something like: ***Mark 3:5-6***, it means it's from the book of Mark, Chapter 3, Verses 5-6.

Similarly, references from the Qur'an are shown with the ***Surah (Chapter)*** followed by the ***Ayat (Verse)***.

Published by CGP

Editors:
Sharon Keeley, Luke von Kotze, Andy Park, Jo Sharrock, Julie Wakeling

Contributors:
Maria Amayuelas-Tann, Jill Hudson, Paul D. Smith

ISBN: 978 1 84762 349 2

With thanks to Mary Falkner for the proofreading.

Scripture quotations (marked NIV) taken from the HOLY BIBLE, NEW INTERNATIONAL VERSION ANGLICISED
Copyright © 1979, 1984, 2011 Biblica, Used by permission of Hodder & Stoughton Ltd, an Hachette UK company
All rights reserved.
"NIV" is a registered trademark of Biblica.
UK trademark number 1448790

Holy Qur'an quotations taken from the Holy Qur'an, Sahih International Version
www.quran.com

Hadith quotations taken from MSA West Compendium of Muslim Texts
www.msawest.net/islam

Quotation on page 34 taken from Decree Ad Gentes, II Vatican Council
Quotations on pages 14 & 22 taken from the Catechism of the Catholic Church

Every effort has been made to locate copyright holders and obtain permission to reproduce sources. For those sources where it has been difficult to trace the originator of the work, we would be grateful for information. If any copyright holder would like us to make an amendment to the acknowledgements, please notify us and we will gladly update the book at the next reprint. Thank you.

Clipart from Corel®
Printed by Elanders Ltd, Newcastle upon Tyne
Based on the classic CGP style created by Richard Parsons.

Text, design, layout and original illustrations © Coordination Group Publications Ltd. (CGP) 2009
All rights reserved.

Photocopying more than one chapter of this book is not permitted. Extra copies are available from CGP.
0870 750 1242 • www.cgpbooks.co.uk

Ethics 1.1 — Religion and Human Relationships

Roles of Men and Women

Christianity, Judaism, Islam & General

As you might have noticed, men and women are _different_ in some ways. Religions have noticed this too...

Roles of Men and Women Have Changed A Lot in Society...

1) In the past, it was seen as a woman's role to take care of the _home_ and raise _children_, while the man went out to _work_. The man was the _head_ of the household, and his wife was expected to be _obedient_.
2) After World War II, these attitudes started to change in the UK. Now it's considered perfectly normal for _women_ to go out to work, and _men_ to take part in housework and childcare (although women still do a lot more of this overall).
3) _Religious views_ on the roles of men and women have shifted in a similar way.

Charles was a modern man — but he just couldn't find where his wife kept the lumps for the gravy.

...And in Christianity

"Wives, submit to your husbands as to the Lord. For the husband is the head of the wife as Christ is the head of the church..."
Ephesians 5:22-23

1) The Bible talks about wives _submitting_ to their husbands (doing as they say).
2) But many Christians argue that this just reflects the ideas of society at that time, and doesn't correspond with _Jesus's attitude_ towards women. Women are found among Jesus's followers, and he treated them _equally_.
3) Nowadays, most Christians believe that men and women should have _equal roles_ in the _family_.

Women have also been treated differently in the Church. For _much_ of the Church's history, women _haven't_ been allowed to be ordained as _priests_. One of the reasons for this is that Jesus only called _men_ to be Apostles. Over the last _50 years_, this has started to _change_ — women can now be ordained as _ministers_ in most Protestant denominations and as _Anglican priests_, but _not_ as Roman Catholic or Orthodox priests. (See p.31)

Mothers are Very Important in Muslim Families

1) In traditional Muslim families, women are generally expected to take care of the _home and the children_, and men are expected to _support_ their wives.

   "Men are in charge of women..." Qur'an 4:34

2) However, it's quite acceptable for women to seek an _education_, or go _out to work_ if their husbands agree.
3) Even though they're not head of the household, _mothers_ have a very _high status_ in Muslim families.

   "...who amongst the people is most deserving of my good treatment? He said: Your mother, again your mother, again your mother, then your father..."
   Prophet Muhammad (Sahih Muslim)

4) _Modern interpretations_ of the teachings of the Qur'an say that husbands should consider what's _normal in society_ when dealing with their wives, and that family decisions should be taken _together_.

The main service in the mosque is on _Friday_, and all males are expected to attend unless they're too ill or travelling. _Women_ don't have to attend the mosque, but if they do they must pray in a _separate_ group from the men. Also, women can't lead men in prayers, but they may lead other women and children. (See p.32)

Jewish Women Must Learn to Run a Jewish Home

1) Jewish women and men have traditional roles in the home. But these expectations are changing, especially for _Reform Jews_ (see p.33).
2) Men and women have _clear roles_ during the _Shabbat meal_ — the mother lights candles and welcomes Shabbat, and the father blesses the children.

There's lots to do to prepare for Shabbat — cleaning the house and preparing food. This was traditionally the woman's job.

There are rules governing _synagogue worship_ too. Usually ten _men_ (called a minyan) are required for a service, and it's _men_ who read from the Torah. Also, in Orthodox synagogues, men and women pray in _separate_ areas. _Reform Jews_ don't accept all these rules, however — women can form a minyan, and even become rabbis.

And in some spider families the male gets eaten...

Religious texts are read within the context of society. And as society changes, they're interpreted differently.

Marriage in Christianity

Christianity

Marriage — a pretty big thing in anyone's life. Including yours if you get a question about it in the exam.

Christians say Marriage Should be Forever

1) The Christian faith values marriage very highly — the joining of husband and wife in holy matrimony reflects the union of Jesus with his followers.
2) Jesus taught that marriage should be a lifelong union — marriage is seen as a covenant or contract between two people, involving commitment and responsibility. Christianity teaches that the purpose of marriage is for two people to offer love and mutual support and for procreation (to have children).
3) Weddings are often events of great importance, with months spent preparing guest lists, clothes, etc.
4) The first step towards getting married is for a couple to get engaged (promise to marry each other). Then a Christian couple would probably go and talk to their priest or minister about their plans.

> "...a man will leave his father and mother and be united to his wife, and the two will become one flesh." Mark 10:7-8

A Christian Wedding has Legal, Social and Religious Features

1) Marriage is a legally recognised relationship between a man and a woman — it gives both certain rights.
2) The ceremony can be 'civil' (non-religious), or religious. Most Christians are married in religious ceremonies that take place in church.
3) The details vary according to tradition and denomination, but all combine legal, social and religious features:

Order of Ceremony
- Hymns
- Opening statement and welcome to friends and family
- Prayers and readings
- Declarations and vows
- Exchanging of rings
- Signing of the register

Hymns symbolise the couple starting their life together with the help of God and the religious community.

These are a traditional part of Christian worship. They remind the couple of the seriousness of their vows.

The rings are a physical symbol of the vows and of lifelong commitment.

Guests symbolise the involvement of the community. The opening statement often explains the purpose of marriage.

The couple declare that there's no reason why they can't marry (and the congregation are asked if they know of any reason why they shouldn't). They then take vows in front of God and the witnesses, which indicates the seriousness and sacredness of marriage.

Signing the marriage register is a legal requirement in the UK.

A Roman Catholic wedding may also include nuptial mass (Holy Communion). In an Orthodox wedding, crowns are placed on the heads of the bride and groom.

Christianity Generally Doesn't Approve of Civil Partnerships

1) Civil partnerships became legal in the UK in December 2005. They give same-sex couples the same rights as married couples concerning things like custody of children.
2) The Bible seems to say that homosexual sex is wrong, but some people (including some priests) argue that the scriptures were written against a different cultural background from ours, and those standards shouldn't be applied today.
3) Even though Christianity no longer condemns homosexuality, it isn't seen as the ideal, and the Church of England doesn't allow same-sex partnerships to be blessed in a church. However, there have been some cases where vicars have gone against this rule and blessed the unions of same-sex couples anyway.

> "Because of this, God gave them over to shameful lusts. Even their women exchanged natural relations for unnatural ones. In the same way the men also abandoned natural relations with women and were inflamed with lust for one another. Men committed indecent acts with other men, and received in themselves the due penalty for their perversion." Romans 1:26-27

RS and marriage — go together like a tidal barrage...

Don't just learn the features of a church wedding — learn how it reflects Christian teachings about marriage.

Ethics 1.1 — Religion and Human Relationships

Marriage in Judaism

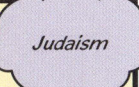
Judaism

Traditionally all Jews have been <u>expected</u> to marry and have at least two children — ideally a boy and a girl.

Marriage Matters in Judaism

1) To Jews, marriage is an <u>emotional</u>, <u>intellectual</u> and <u>spiritual</u> union. It is seen as the proper context for <u>sex</u> (seen as natural and G-d-given) and having children (<u>procreation</u>), but is also for <u>companionship</u>.

2) It's the Jewish custom for parents to arrange for their children to meet suitable partners. To help in this it was common to use a 'shadchan', or <u>matchmaker</u> (and it still is among the ultra-Orthodox).

Nowadays there are shadchan services available via the <u>Internet</u>.

3) Although 40% of UK Jews 'marry out' (i.e. marry non-Jews), those who take their religion seriously find this <u>worrying</u> — children of 'mixed marriages' are less likely to be brought up as <u>observant</u> Jews.

4) When a Jewish couple get engaged, there's a ceremony known as <u>tena'im</u>. In this ceremony, a plate is broken, partly in memory of the destruction of the <u>Temple</u> in Jerusalem in 70 CE. It's said that there can never be complete joy for the Jewish people until the Temple is restored — this is why it's remembered.

5) In the <u>week before the wedding</u>, the groom takes part in a special synagogue service called an <u>ufruf</u> and the bride will immerse herself in a ritual bath called a <u>mikveh</u>, to cleanse herself spiritually before the wedding.

Kiddushin is the First Part of the Marriage Ceremony

'<u>Kiddushin</u>' is the first part of the marriage ceremony, and is usually translated as 'betrothal'. The word comes from a root meaning <u>sanctified</u>, which reflects the <u>holiness</u> of marriage.

Different Jewish communities celebrate marriage in different ways, but there are some <u>common features</u>.

1) The ceremony takes place beneath a <u>chuppah</u>, or wedding <u>canopy</u> — this is a piece of cloth supported by four poles. It is thought that the cloth represents <u>privacy</u>, and the open sides <u>hospitality</u>.

2) Usually, the bride <u>circles</u> the groom <u>seven times</u>. G-d created the world in seven days — so this symbolises the bride building the walls of the couple's new home.

3) The groom gives the bride a <u>ring</u> and makes the <u>betrothal declaration</u>: 'Behold you are consecrated to me with this ring according to the laws of Moses and Israel.' This <u>completes</u> the kiddushin.

4) Then the <u>ketubah</u> (marriage contract) is read out. The traditional ketubah sets out the woman's right to be <u>cared for</u> by her husband, and her entitlements in the event of divorce (a bit like a modern prenuptial agreement). Reform Jews have rewritten the ketubah to be a <u>mutual statement</u> of love and commitment, more like Christian marriage vows. These vows are made before <u>G-d</u>, as well as the <u>congregation</u>.

5) The <u>sheva brachot</u> or <u>seven blessings</u> are said — normally by a rabbi, who usually conducts the service.

6) The groom <u>breaks</u> a glass with his foot to remember the destruction of the Temple (as with the plate at the engagement ceremony).

7) After the service there will be a festive meal and dancing, and shouts of 'mazel tov!' (good luck, best wishes). Among some Orthodox Jews, the men and women dance <u>separately</u>.

Judaism Shares Christianity's Views on Civil Partnerships

1) The Jewish scriptures are basically the same as the Christian Old Testament, so it's no great surprise that Orthodox Judaism holds <u>similar views</u> to Christianity on <u>same-sex couples</u> and <u>civil partnerships</u>.

2) <u>Reform Jews</u> have a more relaxed attitude than Orthodox Jews. They allow <u>commitment ceremonies</u> for homosexuals — these <u>can</u> take place in a synagogue.

Go on, learn it all — and I'll give you a Scooby-snack...

Remember — in religious ceremonies the things that are done aren't just done for a bit of fun. They represent religious beliefs. As with Christianity, Jews believe that marriage should be faithful, and is for having children. Mind you, if religions frowned upon people having children, their followers would eventually all die out.

Ethics 1.1 — Religion and Human Relationships

Marriage in Islam

Islam

Marriage is very important in Islam. Muslims are advised to marry, and Muhammad himself was married.

Marriage in Islam is Recommended for Three Reasons

1) Marriage provides companionship.
2) Marriage provides a secure environment for having children (procreation) and bringing them up as practising Muslims.
3) The sexual instinct is very strong and needs to be carefully channelled.

> "...He created for you from yourselves mates that you may find tranquillity in them; and He placed between you affection and mercy..." Qur'an 30:21

> "Whoever among you can marry, should marry, because it helps him lower his gaze and guard his modesty..." Prophet Muhammad (Sahih Bukhari)

Choosing a Partner is often your Parents' Responsibility

Practising Muslims generally want their children to marry other Muslims. Islam affects a Muslim's whole life, and being married to a non-Muslim could create tension, especially with bringing up children.

1) Most Muslims believe that it's unwise for young men and women to mix freely, and 'dating' is discouraged or even forbidden.
2) In most Muslim communities, parents search for suitable partners for their children — i.e. Muslims often have 'arranged marriages'.
3) Parents also have a responsibility to help if the marriage goes wrong.
4) The marriage contract is considered to be more a 'secular' contract than a religious joining of soulmates by Allah, or a sacrament like in Christianity. This is why both partners must consent to it for it to be valid.
5) The contract gives both the husband and wife rights and responsibilities, but Muslims believe that it'll only work out if the couple respect each other.

The Marriage Ceremony — Customs Vary

The marriage ceremony is different in different Islamic cultures, but there's always a religious ceremony (witnessed by Allah) and a public one (witnessed by the community). They usually go like this...

1) A nikah (contract) is drawn up in advance by the families of the bride and groom, and a mahr (dowry) paid by the groom to the bride.
2) The bride doesn't have to be present — she can send two witnesses in her place.
3) An imam (leader of prayers) is often present (though this isn't compulsory).
4) Vows are exchanged, and a marriage declaration is made by each partner. There may be readings from the Qur'an or a khutbah (speech).
5) There will be a big feast afterwards, though the men and women may enjoy this separately.
6) The marriage ceremony can take place anywhere, although it's usually in a mosque or in the bride or groom's home.

If the venue is in the UK, but isn't registered, the religious ceremony must be followed by a registry office ceremony, so that the marriage will be recognised by the law.

Civil Partnerships are Frowned Upon

1) Homosexuality is strictly forbidden by Islamic Shari'ah law, and in many Muslim countries it's still illegal. In some countries, e.g. Iran and Saudi Arabia, homosexual acts between men carry the death penalty.
2) So Muslims don't approve of same-sex relationships, nor of civil partnerships.

The Qur'an and Hadiths (sayings of the Prophet Muhammad) don't cover every detail of how Muslims should live. Extra day-to-day guidance is found in the law code called the Shari'ah. This is based on Islamic tradition, as well as religious texts, and covers modern issues, such as drugs.

But I never said I wanted to study a foreign language...

Yep — quite a few Arabic words on this page, but the examiner will be really impressed if you use them correctly in your exam. According to Islamic law, Muslim men can have up to four wives (but more on that on page 6). Of course, multiple marriages aren't recognised under British Law. Best get learning this stuff.

Ethics 1.1 — Religion and Human Relationships

Divorce

Christianity, Judaism and Islam

Divorce isn't seen as good by any of the religions. But as 1 in 3 marriages now end in divorce, it's an issue. The religions all teach that God gave everyone free will though — so some things are left to our consciences.

Christian Churches have Different Attitudes to Divorce

1) The breakdown of a marriage involves breaking promises made before God during the marriage ceremony and it's seen by all Christians as a tragedy.
2) Not all Christians agree about whether divorce is permissible, or even possible:

The Roman Catholic Church states that it is actually impossible to divorce. Marriage is a sacrament — God has made the couple into one flesh, and this cannot be undone. However, a marriage can be annulled — annulment means that it was never a true marriage in the first place. This can happen if:
 i) either partner did not consent to the marriage or didn't understand what marriage is about,
 ii) the couple didn't or couldn't have sex, or one partner refused to have children.

Nonconformist Churches (e.g. Baptists and Methodists) will generally remarry divorcees, but an individual minister can refuse to do so if this goes against his or her own conscience.

The Church of England says that divorce is acceptable, but that divorced people can only remarry in church if they can find a minister willing to marry them.

3) Jesus talked about divorce in the Gospels — he was anti-divorce, but pro-forgiveness.

① In Mark 10:2-12 Jesus says that Moses allowed divorce because of people's 'hardness of heart'. But he says that at the Creation of mankind marriages were meant to last for life, and if a divorcee remarries it's the same as adultery.

② Matthew 5:31-32 and 19:8-9 say the same thing — except that divorce is permitted to someone whose partner has already been unfaithful.

③ In John 8:1-11, Jesus freely forgives a woman caught in the act of adultery. But he tells her, 'Go now and leave your life of sin'.

Judaism Isn't Keen on Divorce — But Accepts It

1) Judaism accepts that some marriages don't work out, and that it's better for a couple to divorce than to stay together in bitterness. But divorce is a very last resort after all attempts at reconciliation have failed.
2) Traditionally, a woman cannot initiate divorce, but a divorce does require the wife's consent.
3) In Reform synagogues, if the husband will not grant his wife a certificate of divorce (a 'Get') the Bet Din (Jewish court) can do so, freeing her to remarry.
4) In Orthodox synagogues, women who want a divorce but whose husbands will not grant one (or who aren't around to grant one) are known as 'agunot' — chained women.
5) After the divorce, there are no restrictions on whether the man or woman may remarry.

Divorce is the Last Resort in Islam

1) Divorce is permitted, but only as a very last resort. If things aren't going well, an arbiter from each family should be appointed to try to sort things out.
2) Muslims see reconciliation as particularly important when the couple have children.
3) But, in Islam, marriage is a contract, and like any other contract it can be ended.
4) When the man says 'I divorce you' three times, the marriage is said to be over. However, there's often a period of three months after the first of these declarations. This allows time for reflection, and also to ensure that the woman is not pregnant.
5) A woman can divorce a man in this way (divorce 'by talaq') if it was written into her marriage contract. Otherwise she has to apply to a Shari'ah court (a Muslim religious court) for a divorce 'by khul'.
6) After divorce, both men and women are free to remarry.

"Of all the lawful acts the most detestable to Allah is divorce."
Prophet Muhammad (Sunan Abu Dawud)

This kind of divorce isn't legal in the UK, as Islamic law isn't part of the British legal system.

Yes, dear...

Allegedly, those are the two most important words in a happy marriage. My personal tip for success would be to always let the lady have the biggest wardrobe and the last chocolate in the box...

Ethics 1.1 — Religion and Human Relationships

General

Sexual Relationships

Christianity, Islam and Judaism have all formulated laws concerned with sex. But this doesn't mean that religious people think there's anything wrong or dirty about having sex — quite the opposite.

Christianity, Islam and Judaism have a Lot in Common...

The three faiths have a lot in common when it comes to sex.

1) Traditionally all three religions have taught that the only right context for sexual activity is within marriage. In fact, it's very important to most Muslims that people, especially girls, remain virgins until marriage.
2) The Christian Church teaches that the total giving of self in sex shouldn't be treated casually — self-control and sexual restraint are considered important. Christians are urged to keep sex within marriage for positive reasons more than negative ones — marriage is believed to give sex a special status.
3) Promiscuity (having many sexual partners) is seen as wrong in all three religions — in Christianity it's seen as dishonouring yourself.

...but they're Not Identical

1) Judaism and Christianity are monogamous — adultery (a married person having sex with someone who isn't their husband or wife) is forbidden by the Ten Commandments.
2) Islam permits, but doesn't encourage, polygamy. A man may have up to four wives, but only if he can support them and treat them equally.

> Muhammad actually had eleven wives during his lifetime — although not all at the same time.

3) Some Christians (e.g. monks and Roman Catholic priests) take vows of celibacy — they renounce sex and marriage. They feel it helps them to concentrate on God. Islam and Judaism don't agree with this — they believe that having a family is more important.

Times are Changing Though

1) The number of marriages taking place in the UK each year has been decreasing for at least thirty years.
2) At the same time, it's become more popular (and acceptable) for couples to cohabit (i.e. live together) — either instead of getting married, or as a 'trial marriage' before doing it for real. (However, government statistics seem to show that a marriage is more likely to break down if the couple lived together first.)
3) This means that many people are having sex outside marriage, but within a committed relationship.

Some People Argue That Contraception Makes a Difference

1) Contraception (or birth control) is anything that aims to prevent a woman becoming pregnant (conceiving).
2) Contraception can be temporary (e.g. the contraceptive pill, condoms) or permanent (sterilisation).
3) Modern contraceptives are pretty reliable if used properly, and are freely available in this country.
4) Some liberal Christians, Jews and Muslims feel that the availability of contraception makes it less important that sex is kept strictly within marriage.
5) They argue that when the scriptures were written, contraception was unreliable and the danger of unwanted pregnancy very great.

> Also, allowing sex before marriage gives young people a chance to explore their sexuality and channel their sexual urges. It's argued that sexual frustration is a bad reason to get married.

6) However, 'Orthodox' members of all faiths say that certain moral principles never change.

Sex — the human race would grind to a halt without it...

Even though modern contraception makes unplanned pregnancies less likely, religions all have teachings on whether using it is right or wrong. There's more coming up on this on the next page. Remember, religions regard sex as a gift from God, but one that should only happen in the right circumstance — marriage.

Ethics 1.1 — Religion and Human Relationships

Contraception

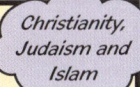

Hmmm... another tricky topic...

Christianity has a Range of Views on Contraception

1) The Roman Catholic Church believes that preventing conception is against the 'natural law' and that the use of any artificial contraception is a grave sin. Indeed, it teaches that humans have an obligation to "Be fruitful and increase in number" (Genesis 1:28).

2) Many individual Roman Catholics disagree with this though, especially because of concerns about AIDS. The Church does allow natural family planning — by only having sex at the times during a woman's cycle when she's less fertile.

3) Other Christian Churches have different views on the matter. The Anglican, Methodist and Presbyterian Churches are in favour of contraception, suggesting that it lets parents plan their family in a responsible way.

4) Many Christians believe that contraception should be a question of individual conscience.

Be fruitful and increase in number...

Islam Teaches that Life is a Sacred Gift from Allah

1) The Qur'an encourages procreation and Muslims believe that conception is the will of Allah. So although contraception isn't specifically mentioned in the Qur'an, it's often seen as unwelcome.

2) Most Muslims feel that it's the right of both husband and wife to try for children, so both partners must agree to any contraception.

"...He gives to whom He wills female [children], and He gives to whom He wills males ...and He renders whom He wills barren..." Qur'an 42:49-50

3) Different Muslims have different views on contraception, e.g. in Iran, contraception for family planning is actively encouraged. But more conservative scholars and clerics have campaigned against contraception.

> In most Muslim countries, contraception is permitted if:
> i) there's a threat to the mother's health,
> ii) it could help a woman who already has children,
> iii) there is a greater than average chance of the child being born with disabilities,
> iv) the family is too poor to raise a child.

4) Only 'reversible' methods are allowed, though — permanent sterilisation and vasectomies are frowned on.

Jews Generally see Contraception as Bad

1) Judaism traditionally teaches that a child is a gift from G-d, and contraception interferes with G-d's plans to bless couples with children.

2) Most Orthodox Jews only accept contraception if pregnancy could be physically or psychologically harmful to the mother or an existing child.

3) Reform Jews are happier with the idea of contraception for family planning — leaving the decision of whether or not to use it to individual conscience. (Having said that, not wanting to have children isn't a good enough reason to use contraception for many Jews.)

4) Sex should be as natural as possible, though, so hormonal contraceptives like the contraceptive pill are generally preferred to barrier methods like condoms. But their use may be encouraged by some as a means of preventing the spread of HIV and other STIs (sexually transmitted infections).

Nothing's ever simple is it...

People interpret their religion's teachings in different ways, so it's difficult to give a clear-cut overview of what a religion teaches. These are very 'human' topics, and people are very different. But all these different opinions about various issues makes for plenty to say in the exam.

Ethics 1.1 — Religion and Human Relationships

Practice Questions

Ding dong, ding dong, ding dong, ding dong... ah, don't you just love weddings. But as with most Ethics topics, it's not all champagne and roses. All three religions teach that marriage involves commitment and faithfulness, and that it's something that has to be worked at...

Speaking of which, it's about time you got to work on some practice questions. Have a go at answering them all. If there are any that you struggle with, go back and have another look at the section. Then try the questions again until you can do them all.
(Have a look at the 'Do Well in Your Exam' and 'Glossary' pages at the back of the book for extra help.)

1) What is:
   a) marriage?
   b) a civil partnership?
   c) procreation?
   d) kiddushin? (Judaism)
   e) the ketubah? (Judaism)
   f) a nikah? (Islam)
   g) a mahr? (Islam)
   h) divorce?
   i) promiscuity?
   j) contraception?

   The glossary at the end of this book is pretty handy for revising for these 1-mark questions.

2) a) State two traditional roles of women in a Christian/Jewish/Muslim family.
   b) Describe Christian/Jewish/Muslim views on civil partnerships.
   c) Describe Christian/Jewish/Muslim beliefs about sex before marriage.

   These questions are just about knowing the basic facts. They're only worth 2 marks each.

3) a) How are the roles of women different from those of men in a traditional church/synagogue/mosque?
   b) Why do Christians/Jews/Muslims consider marriage to be important?
   c) Describe three features of a Christian/Jewish/Muslim marriage ceremony.
   d) Describe Christian/Jewish/Muslim teachings on divorce.
   e) Describe Christian/Jewish/Muslim attitudes to celibacy.

   Make sure you back up your answers to these 3-mark questions with facts. If you can use the specialist vocabulary you've learnt, even better.

4) a) Explain Christian/Jewish/Muslim attitudes to the roles of men and women in society.
   b) Explain how a Christian/Jewish/Muslim wedding ceremony reflects religious teachings about marriage.
   c) Explain different Christian beliefs about divorce. (Christianity)
   d) Explain why some Christians/Jews/Muslims are against the use of contraception.

   For these questions, you're marked on the quality of your writing, as well as what you know. They're worth 6 marks each, so you need to spend a bit of time on them.

5) Read the following statements:
   a) "Marriage is important."
   b) "Civil partnerships shouldn't be allowed."
   c) "Getting a divorce is better than living in an unhappy marriage."
   d) "Divorced people should never be allowed to remarry."
   e) "Religious couples should keep sex within marriage."
   Discuss each statement. You should include different, supported points of view and a personal viewpoint. You must refer to a religion in your answer.

   Write your answers to these questions in proper sentences. They are worth 12 marks in the exam, with extra marks available for good spelling, punctuation and grammar.

Ethics 1.1 — Religion and Human Relationships

Abortion

Abortion is a subject that people often hold very strong views about.
And, as you'd probably expect, religious believers often have strong views about it too.

Abortion — Terminating a Pregnancy

1) Abortion is when a foetus is removed prematurely from the womb, before it is able to survive.
2) Abortion can legally take place in the UK until the 24th week of pregnancy, as long as two doctors agree that it's required. They must consider the quality of life of the woman, the unborn child, and any children the mother may already have.

> There are complicated arguments for and against abortion...
> i) The 'pro-choice' argument says that a woman has the right to choose what happens to her body (and since the foetus isn't independent of the woman, this argument says it must be considered part of the woman).
> ii) But is it right to consider the foetus part of the mother when it's genetically different?
> iii) Although many people are generally against abortion (seeing it as the taking of a life) they will agree that in certain circumstances, abortion should be permitted, e.g. if the mother's or child's health is at risk, if a woman has become pregnant through rape, or if a mother is too young to cope with a child.
> iv) The question of when life actually begins is important here, too. Is it at conception (as the Roman Catholic Church says)? Or at birth? And is a foetus an actual person, or just a potential person?

Many Christians see Abortion as Undesirable

1) Abortion is a very complicated and emotional issue, but generally speaking, Christianity teaches that abortion is undesirable. However, the Roman Catholic Church goes so far as to say that abortion is murder.
2) Not all Christian churches see it in such 'black-and-white' terms, however. The Church of England view is that abortion is permissible in certain circumstances, while the Religious Society of Friends (the Quakers) argues that the life of the unborn child cannot be valued above that of the woman.
3) Indeed, many Christians argue that allowing a woman to choose is a way of showing Christian compassion — whether they agree with the choice made or not.

> "Abortion has been considered to be murder since the first centuries of the Church, and nothing permits it to be considered otherwise."
> Pope Paul VI (Leader of Roman Catholic Church, 1970)

The 'Sanctity of Life' Argument

> Probably the most important biblical passage regarding the Sanctity of Life argument is the sixth of the Ten Commandments, "You shall not murder." Exodus 20:13

1) Because the Bible says that we were created in the image of God and given the gift of life, many Christians believe that we do not have the right to interfere with when life ends, or to prevent the beginning of a new life.
2) Although the Bible doesn't actually mention abortion, other Christian writings (e.g. the Didache, a 2nd century manual of Christian teaching) are quite specifically against it.

It's tricky, emotional stuff...

There are no easy answers. So learn the stuff on this page, and be ready to give both sides of the argument.

Abortion: Judaism and Islam

Judaism & Islam

Abortion is a tricky issue for any religion — it's worthwhile remembering that there are pretty good reasons for having very different opinions.

Jews Generally see Abortion as Bad

1) There are no direct teachings about abortion in the Torah, so Jews rely on Rabbinical teachings from the Talmud, and on interpreting Torah verses about similar issues.
2) Exodus 21:22-25 sets out the punishment for men who, while fighting, accidentally strike a pregnant woman. If they cause her to give birth prematurely (usually taken to mean a miscarriage) the penalty is a fine. If the woman is seriously hurt or killed then the ruling is 'an eye for an eye'.

> "If men who are fighting hit a pregnant woman and she gives birth prematurely but there is no serious injury, the offender must be fined... But if there is serious injury, you are to take life for life..." Exodus 21:22-23

3) Most Jews take this to mean that, although the accidental killing of a foetus is wrong, it's not equivalent to murder. Many Jews extend this rule to deliberate abortion.
4) The Talmud teaches that the life of an unborn child is not as valuable as that of the mother, and if a pregnancy puts the life of the mother at risk, it must be terminated.
5) Some Rabbis will also allow an abortion if the pregnancy is mentally dangerous for the mother, or if the child will be severely disabled. But it cannot simply be carried out for convenience.
6) The later in the pregnancy abortion is requested, the more difficult it becomes for Judaism to allow it.
7) Orthodox Jews will tend to be against abortion in most cases, whereas Reform Jews tend to place the final decision with the mother.

The Qur'an says: Do Not Kill Your Children...

1) The passage on the right sums up Islamic teaching on abortion.
2) It certainly isn't welcomed, although there are circumstances in which abortion may be permissible.

> "And do not kill your children... Indeed, their killing is ever a great sin." Qur'an 17:31

> "Then He proportioned him and breathed into him from His [created] soul and made for you hearing and vision and hearts; little are you grateful." Qur'an 32:9

3) Muslims don't believe that the foetus is fully human until it receives its soul.
4) Most schools of Islamic thought place this date between 40 days and 120 days after conception. But all Muslims believe that the foetus is 'alive' from the moment of conception.
5) Some schools of Islam allow abortion before 120 days if there's a serious reason for it, e.g. if the foetus carries a serious illness that would make the child's life very difficult or painful, or if the pregnancy was the result of rape.
6) Other Muslim authorities believe that abortion in these circumstances is always wrong.
7) However, at any date, if the mother's life is in danger, abortion is seen as lawful. The potential life in the womb is not as important as the actual life of the mother.
8) The loss of the unborn child is seen as a lesser evil than the loss of the mother, who most likely has a husband and may have other children to take care of.
9) Some Muslim women argue that they should be free to choose what happens to their bodies. Those that disagree claim that in the Qur'an it says that unborn children will want to know why they were killed.

Don't expect everyone to agree any time soon...

Although you need to be able to express your own opinion in the exam, the ideal would be that you could express the opposite opinion as clearly as if it was your own. If you're not totally sure what to believe about these issues, you'll just have to pick one side of the debate to agree with for the sake of the exam.

Fertility Treatment

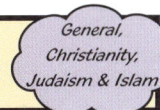
General, Christianity, Judaism & Islam

There are many similarities in the attitudes of Christians, Muslims and Jews towards fertility treatment. All believe that a child is a gift, and therefore all allow some methods of fertility treatment.

Infertility means an Inability to Conceive a Child

Nowadays, there are various kinds of fertility treatment that can be used to help.

   Artificial Insemination by the Husband (AIH) — sperm from the husband is injected into the wife's womb.
   Artificial Insemination by Donor (AID) — sperm from a sperm bank (i.e. an anonymous donor) is used.
   In Vitro Fertilisation (IVF) — eggs are fertilised in a test tube and 1 or 2 are implanted in the mother's womb.
   Egg Donation — where an egg from a different woman is used.
   Cloning — a possible future technique for creating children genetically identical to one parent.

Christianity sees Children as a Blessing from God

1) Most Christian Churches believe that it's okay for science to help childless couples to conceive — as long as the process doesn't involve anyone else.
2) So AIH is permissible. The couple can be blessed with a child, and the sanctity of marriage isn't interfered with. Many Roman Catholics still aren't keen though, since the sperm comes from an 'unnatural' sex act.
3) Some Christians believe that if AIH fails, a couple should adopt instead. Though many other Christians consider IVF an appropriate treatment if the wife's egg and husband's sperm are used.
4) AID and egg donation are much less favoured methods, since a 'third party' is involved.
5) The Roman Catholic Church is opposed to IVF in all forms, as it often creates 'spare' embryos that are thrown away. Many Catholics argue that life begins at fertilisation, and that even an embryo has rights.
6) Most Christians oppose cloning, seeing it as a human attempt to 'play God'. Some object that many foetuses will die developing the technique, and that each child is meant to be unique.

Muslims allow some Fertility Treatments

1) Again, some scientific methods are permissible, as long as all natural methods of conceiving have failed.
2) Artificial insemination and IVF are both okay, as long as the egg of the wife and the sperm of the husband are used. But AID is not acceptable as the sperm is donated. Many Muslims see this as a sin comparable with adultery, as the woman has become pregnant using the sperm of a man other than her husband.
3) There are also concerns about diseases that could be inherited from an anonymous sperm donor (although most sperm banks screen donors for serious genetic disorders).
4) Shi'ite Muslims sometimes allow egg donation, so long as the donor is a Muslim woman, and there's no other way for the couple to have a child.
5) Most Muslims see cloning as wrong, as it tries to take over Allah's role in creation. Others think that if it took place within marriage there'd be no reason to ban it, as it would rely on Allah's will for it to be successful.

Judaism allows most Methods

"Be fruitful and increase in number; fill the earth..."
Genesis 1:28

1) In Jewish teaching, there's an emphasis on having a family.
2) So it's left to individual married couples to decide whether or not to use scientific methods of conception.
3) A Jewish couple might seek advice on the matter from their rabbi (religious leader).
4) AIH is usually permitted, but not AID, as the use of donated sperm might be seen as a form of adultery.
5) IVF is generally approved of — as long as the egg and the sperm are from the married couple involved.
6) Egg donation is seen as okay, though the couple will often prefer the egg to come from a Jewish woman. This is because, according to Orthodox teachings, you're only a Jew if your mother is a Jew.
7) The idea of cloning isn't considered bad in Judaism. Many Jews think that if there's no other way for a man to reproduce (men are obliged to try to have at least two children) reproductive cloning would be acceptable.

Putting fertiliser on it won't help...

Not being able to have children can be heartbreaking for a couple. If the technology exists to have a child, but their religion is against using it, what should they do? Tricky...

Ethics 1.2 — Religion and Medical Ethics

Euthanasia and Suicide

General & Christianity

Another couple of very complicated subjects...

Euthanasia is often called Mercy Killing

> Euthanasia means killing someone painlessly to relieve suffering, especially from an incurable illness. It's often called mercy killing.

1) There are two forms of euthanasia — voluntary euthanasia and non-voluntary euthanasia.
2) Voluntary euthanasia is when an ill person actively requests assistance to die, or refuses treatment which is keeping them alive, i.e. the person decides that they want to die and seeks help to achieve this.
3) Non-voluntary euthanasia is when the patient is unable to make such a request, and the decision is made by someone else — usually doctors and family members.
4) Suicide is when someone takes their own life — often because of illness, for example depression or terminal cancer. Attempted suicide used to be a crime in the UK, but it's now seen as a sign that someone needs help.
5) Assisted suicide is when a doctor provides someone with the means to end their own life, usually by prescribing a lethal dose of medication.

Euthanasia is Illegal in the UK

1) Euthanasia and assisted suicide are illegal in the UK, but euthanasia is allowed in certain circumstances in Albania, Belgium, Luxembourg, and the Netherlands, and assisted suicide is legal in Switzerland.
2) The charity 'Dignity in Dying' believes that many people would be grateful for 'the mercy of a painless death', and many people want assisted suicide legalised in the UK. In the 2005 British Social Attitudes Survey, 80% of people said that they were in favour of letting terminally ill patients die with a doctor's help.
3) Legalisation would mean that scarce medical resources could be saved for people who could be cured.
4) A few doctors have even admitted to helping patients to die, sometimes by giving a patient an excess of painkillers, which can ease suffering but can also lead to eventual death — this is known as 'double effect', which is legal so long as the intention was to relieve pain.
5) However, there is a concern that if euthanasia were legalised, some elderly people may feel under pressure to end their life, even if they don't want to.

"Your Body is a Temple of the Holy Spirit"

1) The passage in the subheading (from 1 Corinthians NIV) suggests that God lives within each of us. Life is considered a sacred gift, and so both euthanasia and suicide are seen as wrong by many Christians (see page 9 — the 'Sanctity of Life' argument). However, some argue that Jesus's resurrection proves that death is not the end, and that earthly life isn't always the most important thing.
2) Roman Catholics are the most strongly opposed to euthanasia. They believe that anything that intentionally causes death is 'a grave violation of the law of God'. So even those who are unlikely to recover consciousness should be kept alive.
3) To Roman Catholics, suicide is considered so grave a sin that suicides aren't given a Christian burial. However, some Christians point out passages in the Bible that describe suicide (e.g. King Saul's death in 1 Samuel 31:4-5) without calling it a sin.
4) Many Christians suggest that the easing of suffering in euthanasia is a way of demonstrating Christian compassion, and that the use of 'extraordinary treatment' (e.g. life-support machines) to keep a person alive is not always the best approach.
5) Most Anglican denominations agree that terrible distress should not be suffered at all costs, and that death may be considered a blessing. They argue that a person's quality of life must also be considered.
6) Local churches often have links with hospices. A hospice is a place where terminally ill people can be cared for, and can discuss any fears that they may have about death.

I told you it was complicated...

While religions provide clear guidelines on many matters, there doesn't seem to be much clear-cut teaching on medical ethics. It comes down to interpreting scripture and tradition to try to find what's right.

Ethics 1.2 — Religion and Medical Ethics

Euthanasia and Suicide

Judaism & Islam

Religions don't shy away from giving guidance on the big issues.

Jews Believe Only G-d should Decide when we Die

1) Jewish teaching is, generally, opposed to the practice of euthanasia — life is seen as a gift from God and is therefore sacred. We do not have the right to decide when a life should end.

2) The same thing applies to suicide — most Jews see it as such a great sin that those who take their own lives are not buried in the same part of the cemetery as other Jews.

3) However, most Jews who are suspected of having committed suicide are given standard funeral rites, as they are often judged to have been disturbed beyond being responsible for their actions.

4) The relief of pain and suffering is a key part of Jewish teaching. So although euthanasia is seen as wrong if it involves actively doing something to cause someone's death, it may be possible to withhold treatment, if this treatment was causing further distress.

5) The words of Rabbi Moses Isserles are sometimes used to argue that it may be reasonable to switch off a life-support machine that's keeping someone alive.

"If there is anything which causes a hindrance to the departure of the soul... then it is permissible to remove it."

Islam Teaches that Life is a Sacred Gift from Allah

1) Muslims believe that Allah created the world and everything in it. Our lives are sacred, and only Allah can decide when a life may end or when it may begin.

2) This means that suicide and euthanasia are generally seen as wrong.

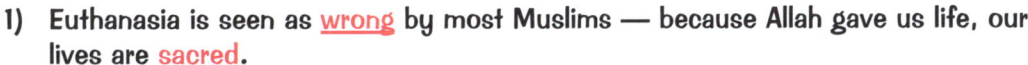

"And it is not [possible] for one to die except by permission of Allah at a decree determined..." Qur'an 3:145

Allah knows Why we Suffer...

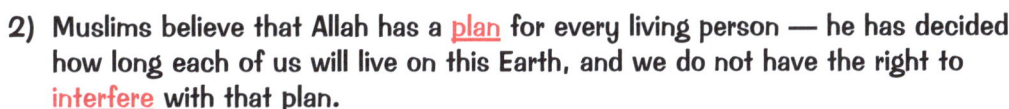

Allah even has a plan for you, Norman Shuffleploppy.

1) Euthanasia is seen as wrong by most Muslims — because Allah gave us life, our lives are sacred.

2) Muslims believe that Allah has a plan for every living person — he has decided how long each of us will live on this Earth, and we do not have the right to interfere with that plan.

3) Islam teaches that life on Earth is a test. Allah knows why we suffer, and we do not have good reason to end our own lives, no matter how bad that suffering becomes.

4) Instead, those who are suffering should turn to Allah, pray and 'patiently persevere' — Allah is merciful, and all will be revealed on the Day of Judgement.

5) However, in cases where a patient may have terminal illness with no hope of improvement, Islam allows doctors to stop 'unnecessary' treatment.

6) In cases where somebody is on a life-support machine, it may be allowable to switch this off if the damage is such that there is no hope of recovery.

Learn this page — then go do something cheery...

Hopefully you'll never have to face any of these issues anywhere other than in a religious studies exam. Religions have something to say about all the stages of people's lives, from the beginning to the very end — and not just when everything goes to plan. None of the religions promise anyone an easy time.

Ethics 1.2 — Religion and Medical Ethics

Using Animals in Medical Research

Christianity, Judaism & Islam

Religions usually say be nice to other people. But what about squirrels...

Christianity says Animals come Below People

According to the Bible, God created the world, mankind was created to populate it, and animals were created for the use of mankind. But animal rights issues are still of interest to many Christians.

1) One of the major issues for Christians is whether animals have souls or not. Many people believe that animals don't have souls, meaning that God created us as superior to them. Some people argue that animals are here for our use.

2) Christianity teaches that we should treat animals with kindness, but that they can be used to benefit mankind (as long as their suffering is considered). It's also thought that excessive money shouldn't be 'wasted' on animals when human beings are suffering. So humans are very definitely 'on top', with animals below.

> "...Rule over the fish of the sea and the birds of the air and over every living creature that moves on the ground." *Genesis 1:28*

3) The Roman Catholic Church tolerates animal experimentation, but only if it brings benefit to mankind (e.g. if the experiments lead to the development of life-saving medicines). The Catechism of the Roman Catholic Church (paragraph 2417) says that animal experimentation is allowable so long as it "remains within reasonable limits and contributes to caring for or saving human lives."

4) But some Christians think that it's always wrong to cause suffering to animals just to increase our scientific knowledge — particularly since medicines don't always have the same effect on humans as they do on animals.

5) There are some Christian organisations who campaign for greater compassion to be shown to animals, such as the group Catholic Concern for Animals.

6) Some Christians point out that as everything is interdependent, our treatment of animals reflects on us. Indeed, the Church of England teaches that the medical and technological use of animals should be monitored 'in the light of ethical principles'.

Judaism Forbids Cruelty to Animals

1) The Noahide Laws (given to Noah after the Flood) clearly forbid cruelty to animals. Animals are here to help us, and not to be abused.

2) There are many passages in the Torah that demonstrate care for animals.

> *Deuteronomy 5:14* says that animals deserve a day off on the Sabbath, just like people.

3) But most of the commandments in the Torah can be broken if it is to save human life.

4) This means that animal testing to develop life-saving drugs is acceptable. However, it should only be carried out as a last resort, and without resulting in any unnecessary pain for the animals involved.

Islam calls for Animals to be Treated Humanely

1) Khalifah is the idea that we're responsible for the Earth — Khalifah means Vice-Regent, or Trustee.

2) Cruelty to animals is forbidden, as is their use simply for our pleasure. Islam teaches that we'll have to answer on the Day of Judgement for any ill-treatment of animals.

3) Muslims believe in demonstrating mercy and compassion for all living creatures.

4) Muslims will generally only allow animal testing if it is done to produce genuine medical advances for humans. The animals should be treated humanely, and no unnecessary pain should be inflicted on them.

You might be tested on animal testing...

All three of these religions think that people come first, but that animals should be treated well. The difficult bit is how to decide when it's acceptable for an animal to suffer if it benefits humans. The general consensus is that if it's for medical research, and the welfare of the animal is always kept in mind, then it's probably OK.

Ethics 1.2 — Religion and Medical Ethics

Practice Questions

Quite a 'heavy' section this one, but you have to treat it like any other section. Make sure you know what the religious teachings are on each issue, and why some people might disagree with them.

To help you along in the learning process, here are some questions for you to have a go at. They're eerily similar to the ones you'll face in the exam, so they're good practice. Keep repeating them until you're awesomely confident.

1) What is:
   a) abortion?
   b) infertility?
   c) egg donation?
   d) cloning?
   e) euthanasia?
   f) a hospice?

   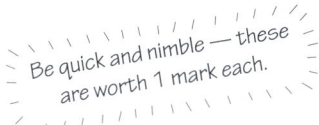
   Be quick and nimble — these are worth 1 mark each.

2) a) What is meant by the 'sanctity of life' argument?
   b) Describe Christian/Jewish/Muslim attitudes to cloning.
   c) What is the difference between suicide and euthanasia?

   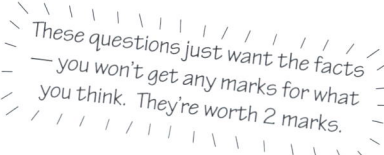
   These questions just want the facts — you won't get any marks for what you think. They're worth 2 marks.

3) a) Describe Christian/Jewish/Muslim teachings on abortion.
   b) Explain why some Christians are against in vitro fertilisation. (Christianity)
   c) Describe Christian/Jewish/Muslim teachings on euthanasia.
   d) Why do many Christians/Jews/Muslims reject the use of animal testing in non-medical research?

   3 marks each. Make sure you read the questions properly.

4) a) Explain how the sanctity of life argument affects some Christians' beliefs about abortion. (Christianity)
   b) Explain why Christianity/Judaism/Islam allows some forms of fertility treatment but not others.
   c) Explain why some Christians/Jews/Muslims will allow abortion in some cases.
   d) Explain why some Christians/Jews/Muslims may feel it is not wrong to withhold medical treatment in cases where a patient is not expected to get better.
   e) Explain why most Christians/Jews/Muslims would expect animals being used for medical research to be treated humanely.

   There are 6 marks available for each of these. You'll get more marks if you use specialist terms.

5) Read the following statements:
   a) "Abortion is wrong in all circumstances."
   b) "People should be allowed to use any type of fertility treatment to help them have children."
   c) "Euthanasia is wrong in all circumstances."
   d) "Animal testing for medicines should be allowed."

   Discuss each statement. You should include different, supported points of view and a personal viewpoint. You must refer to a religion in your answer.

   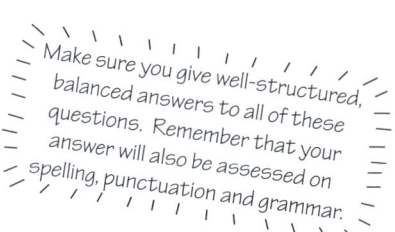
   Make sure you give well-structured, balanced answers to all of these questions. Remember that your answer will also be assessed on spelling, punctuation and grammar.

Ethics 1.2 — Religion and Medical Ethics

Ethics 1.3 — Religion, Poverty and Wealth

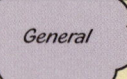 General

Wealth, Poverty and Disease

Wealth is basically money and possessions. Wealth is a big issue for religious people, because it's not very evenly distributed in society — some people are rolling in it, while other people are left struggling in poverty.

Being Wealthy isn't a Bad Thing in Itself

1) None of the three major religions teach that wealth is bad.
2) There are people in the Bible who are both wealthy and faithful to God, e.g. Joseph of Arimathea was a rich council member who retrieved the body of Jesus from the Roman authorities and arranged his burial.
3) And there are plenty of examples from the Jewish books of the Kings, e.g. King Solomon was one of the great kings of Israel, who built the Temple in Jerusalem: "King Solomon was greater in riches and wisdom than all the other kings of the earth." (1 Kings 10:23)
4) Muslims believe that all wealth belongs to Allah, and that personal wealth is a gift from Allah.
5) So in all three religions, it's not wealth, but a love of wealth that's a problem:

"...there came a rich man from Arimathea, named Joseph, who had himself become a disciple of Jesus." Matthew 27:57

"No one can serve two masters... You cannot serve both God and Money." Matthew 6:24

"...those who hoard gold and silver and spend it not in the way of Allah — give them tidings of a painful punishment." Qur'an 9:34

"Whoever loves money never has money enough..." Ecclesiastes 5:10

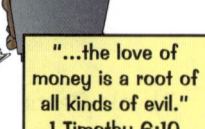

"...the love of money is a root of all kinds of evil." 1 Timothy 6:10

There are Many Causes of Poverty and Hunger

Poverty leads to great suffering. So its causes and effects are of great concern for religious people.

1) The Brandt Report in 1980 identified an imbalance between the developed and the developing worlds. The developed world contains around 25% of the world's population but around 80% of the wealth. Little has changed since 1980. Some religious people believe that the greed of people in developed countries leads to poverty in developing countries.
2) Direct causes of poverty in the developing world include rapid population growth, war, and the sale of raw materials at low prices. This poverty often leads to hunger, because people can't afford to buy food.
3) Famine, an overall lack of food in an area, is often caused by war or climate. War stops people from working on farms, because they're either involved in the fighting or sheltering from the violence. Droughts, floods and other extreme weather conditions can destroy crops and ruin the fertility of the soil.
4) Hundreds of thousands of people die of starvation every year.
5) In the UK, causes of poverty range from unemployment to gambling and alcoholism. The poorest people become homeless and are dependent on charity for food and shelter.

Poverty and Disease Often Go Together

1) Poverty and disease are very closely related. The effects of poverty, e.g. malnutrition, poor sanitation, lack of proper healthcare, etc. leave people more susceptible to disease — particularly children. The World Health Organisation estimates that around a third of all deaths worldwide are poverty related.
2) At the same time, disease weakens people, making it harder for them to work their way out of poverty.
3) Education also has an effect on patterns of disease. For example, sexually transmitted diseases like HIV and syphilis can be controlled by educating people about safe sex and avoiding promiscuity.
4) Religious organisations like Christian Aid, Muslim Aid and the Jewish charity Tzedek, aim to provide immediate help for the sick and starving, as well as long-term projects to help whole communities get themselves out of poverty. (More about that on the next three pages.)

Money makes the world go round, the world go round...

People used to believe that disease was sent by God as a punishment for sin. This attitude still existed as recently as the start of the AIDS epidemic. Since the disease first took root in the gay community, some religious people believed that AIDS was a punishment for the sin of homosexuality.

Money and Charity: Christianity

Christianity

Basically, Christianity teaches that you shouldn't be selfish with your money.

It's What You Do With Your Money that Counts

1) Christians believe you should only earn money in moral ways (see p.20).
2) Also, you mustn't use your money in ways that might harm you or others.
3) This means many Christians (especially Methodists) disapprove of gambling (playing games of chance for money). Gambling can be addictive, and profits are made at the expense of others.
4) Christians also disapprove of the practice of usury — charging high rates of interest on loans. This is seen as profiting from someone else's poverty.
5) Most Christians do accept interest on loans, as long as it's charged at a reasonable level. But some Christians consider moneylending to be an immoral occupation.

The Roman Catholic Church and to a lesser extent the Church of England are very rich institutions — this is a worry for some believers.

Christians have a Duty to be Charitable

1) Jesus taught that the most important commandments were to love God and to "love your neighbour as yourself" (Mark 12:31). For Christians, charity means putting this love into practice:

> "If anyone has material possessions and sees his brother in need but has no pity on him, how can the love of God be in him? ...let us not love with words or tongue but with actions and in truth." 1 John 3:17-18

2) Christians believe they have a duty to care for other people, and use many sources of authority to stress this. The Bible contains many passages encouraging charity.

> "The man with two tunics should share with him who has none, and the one who has food should do the same." Luke 3:11

> "Go, sell everything you have and give to the poor, and you will have treasure in heaven." Mark 10:21

> "I was hungry and you gave me something to eat, I was thirsty and you gave me something to drink... whatever you did for one of the least of these brothers of mine, you did for me." Matthew 25:35-40

3) In practice, 'charity' is any sort of help that's freely given. This could be a donation of time (e.g. visiting the sick or elderly), effort (e.g. working on a building project) or material things (e.g. giving money). A number of Christian charities exist — working both in the UK and globally, e.g. Christian Aid:

CHRISTIAN AID

Christian Aid was set up after World War II to help refugees. It now has over 40 member organisations in the UK and Ireland, and works globally to relieve poverty. It raises money through donations, events and collections.

Most of Christian Aid's work is in development — they believe the best way to help people is by 'helping them to help themselves'. They set up projects in the developing world, drawing on the skills of local people.

Development projects set up by Christian Aid aim to help with problems such as poor sanitation, education and healthcare, as well as encouraging the use of birth control. The organisation also aims to change government policy to help reduce the suffering of the world's poor, e.g. through debt relief, and fair-trade products.

4) Some religious orders (communities of monks or nuns) are dedicated to relieving suffering amongst the starving, poor and sick. One example is the Order of the Missionaries of Charity:

MOTHER TERESA

Mother Teresa was an Albanian Roman Catholic nun who devoted herself to the destitute and dying in Calcutta, India. She founded the Order of the Missionaries of Charity, whose nuns now work amongst the poor all over the world. She said that it isn't what you do for God that counts, but how much love you pour into it. She won the Nobel Peace Prize in 1979, and died in 1997 at the age of 87.

Feel the luuurve...

Christians don't have any strict rules about how much of their income they should give to the poor (although many use 10% as a guideline). Donations are left to the conscience of each individual Christian. Jesus emphasised that you should give charitably out of love, rather than because society expects it of you.

Money and Charity: Judaism

Judaism

Judaism teaches that it's our duty to look after those less fortunate than ourselves, and Jews are expected to give some of their income to the poor and needy.

Jews must Deal Fairly and Honestly

1) Although Judaism doesn't teach that everyone should try to be wealthy, it does suggest that extreme poverty will make others responsible for you — all Jews should aim to work and earn a living.
2) But the love of wealth may turn you from G-d — so you should neither seek nor shun wealth.
3) Unfairness and dishonesty in business are condemned — you're answerable to G-d for any wrongdoing.
4) It's also strictly forbidden for one Jew to charge interest on a loan to another Jew (Leviticus 25:37) — a practice called 'usury'. This rule doesn't apply to loans made to non-Jews: "You may charge a foreigner interest, but not a brother Israelite..." (Deuteronomy 23:20).

> "Hear this, you who trample the needy and do away with the poor of the land... skimping the measure, boosting the price and cheating with dishonest scales... The LORD has sworn by the Pride of Jacob: 'I will never forget anything they have done.'" Amos 8:4-7

5) Although gambling is generally frowned on, occasional lighthearted games for small stakes are allowed. For example, it's traditional to play a gambling game called kvitlech (similar to blackjack) at Hanukkah.
6) Jews try to avoid talking about or handling money on the Sabbath — the day of rest.

Judaism says, "Do not be hardhearted or tightfisted..."

1) This passage from Deuteronomy sums up Jewish teaching on charity:

> "If there is a poor man among your brothers in any of the towns of the land... do not be hardhearted or tightfisted toward your poor brother." Deuteronomy 15:7

2) Also, Maimonides said that the best way to give was "to help a person help themselves so that they may become self-supporting".

Maimonides was an important Jewish Rabbi and philosopher.

3) There are two main ways of giving to charity — Tzedakah and Gemilut Hasadim:

> **TZEDAKAH:** Tzedakah is financial aid — even the poorest in society are expected to contribute 10% of their wealth. All wealth belongs to G-d, and not giving to the poor deprives them of what they're owed.
>
> **GEMILUT HASADIM:** This means, literally, the 'giving of loving-kindness' and refers to any kind and compassionate actions towards others.

4) Many Jewish homes have collection boxes (called pushkes) in which money for charity can be placed. Children are encouraged to use these boxes — maybe donating some of their pocket money each week.
5) Donating clothing to people who need it, feeding the hungry, visiting someone who's sick and burying the dead are all considered Gemilut Hasadim. The most important thing is that, whatever you're giving, you don't expect anything in return.
6) There are Jewish charities that have been set up to help the poor:

> **TZEDEK (JEWISH ACTION FOR A JUST WORLD)**
> Tzedek is a Jewish charity set up in the UK that works with poor people of all races and religions, 'providing direct support to small scale sustainable self-help development projects for the relief and elimination of poverty'.
>
> Their focus is on helping local projects, e.g. health and agriculture training schemes, that improve a community's ability to get itself out of poverty and achieve a better standard of living.

Not many Jews in Yorkshire then — sorry, sorry... ...I'll get my coat

Judaism teaches that G-d has provided the world with everything we need, so that there should never be any poverty or hunger. Jews believe that the poverty that does exist is caused by the greed of others.

Ethics 1.3 — Religion, Poverty and Wealth

Money and Charity: Islam

In Islam, the principle is much the same as Christianity and Judaism — greed and waste are frowned upon.

Gambling and Charging Interest are Absolute No-Nos

1) Islam forbids using money in ways that might damage yourself or others — it's a basic principle of Shari'ah (Islamic law) that a Muslim should not harm others.
2) If you win money by gambling, it's only because someone else has lost it.
3) Shari'ah also forbids any financial deals involving the charging of interest. This is to prevent rich people making more money at the expense of poorer people, and to make sure wealth is spread more fairly.

Charging interest (particularly a high rate of interest) is called usury. The Arabic word for it is riba.

4) This means Muslims can't use most Western bank accounts. Also, Muslim businesses must be run differently from others, because the Western economic system depends on lending money and charging interest. Some Islamic banks exist to get around this.

Charity is One of the Five Pillars of Islam

1) Muslims believe that possessions ultimately belong to Allah.
2) Islam teaches that you should act responsibly and help those in need.
3) As in Judaism, there are two main ways to help the disadvantaged — Zakah and Sadaqah:

> **ZAKAH:** This is one of the Five Pillars of Islam — 2.5% of your yearly savings should be given to the needy, no matter how rich or poor you are.
> **SADAQAH:** This is additional aid — maybe financial donations or an act of compassion and love.

4) Zakah is the Third Pillar of Islam. The Five Pillars are a guide to living a good Muslim life — they're practical ways of showing obedience to Allah. Zakah is also a way of redistributing wealth.
   - The money donated is collected by a local mosque. It's then redistributed to needy Muslims, or used for religious purposes, like running Muslim schools.
   - It's a sign of concern for others and encourages unselfishness.
5) This Hadith (saying of the Prophet Muhammad) sums up the importance of Zakah pretty clearly:

> "Whoever is made wealthy by Allah and does not pay the Zakah of his wealth, then on the Day of Resurrection his wealth will be made like a bald-headed poisonous male snake with two black spots over the eyes. The snake will encircle his neck and bite his cheeks and say, 'I am your wealth, I am your treasure.'" — Prophet Muhammad (Sahih Bukhari)

6) There are Islamic charities, that help the poor globally and in the UK — e.g. Muslim Aid and Islamic Aid.

MUSLIM AID
Muslim Aid provides disaster relief and development aid around the world.
They aim to provide not only initial emergency aid after a war or natural disaster, but ongoing help to get people back on their feet. This help includes building new permanent housing, sanitation and schools, and offering small interest-free loans to help start-up businesses.

ISLAMIC AID
Islamic Aid is an international organisation dedicated to reducing poverty and deprivation.
In the UK, they work to improve the lives of Muslim immigrants, e.g. by raising awareness of 'ghettos'.

Don't gamble on this in the exam — get it learnt...

Muslim businesses still need money to start up, and this can be a problem without business loans. Often, a Muslim will look for an investor instead, who becomes part of the business rather than just a lender.

Ethics 1.3 — Religion, Poverty and Wealth

Moral and Immoral Occupations

General

'Morality' is about what's 'right' and what's 'wrong'. Or, from a religious point of view, what God does and doesn't approve of. Christians, Muslims and Jews all believe there are moral and immoral ways to make money.

Challenging Behaviour — Absolute and Relative Morality

Religious people don't always agree about how (if at all) they should try to influence the conduct of society.

1) Some people consider it wrong to 'impose their morals on others' — while some think it's wrong to sit by and 'watch society go down the drain'.
2) This is why some religious people campaign vigorously against what they see as immoral occupations — while others would prefer to let people make up their own minds. They believe it's more effective to show compassion than to act like a moral police force.
3) Also, some people strongly support the idea of absolute morality, which means that they think many things are always right or always wrong.
4) Others favour relative morality, which holds that most things are sometimes right and sometimes wrong, depending on the circumstances.

Sigh... if only everyone were like me...

Some Occupations are Generally Considered Immoral

The occupations that are generally considered immoral by all three faiths are those that exploit or harm other people, are damaging to the environment, or are sexual in nature.

EXPLOITATIVE OR HARMFUL OCCUPATIONS:
The most obvious examples are illegal ways of making money, e.g. theft, blackmail and drug trafficking. They're directly harmful to other people, and so are strictly forbidden.

Most religious people would also consider it immoral to work in a casino or make gambling equipment, since they're encouraging people to gamble. Some, particularly certain Christians, think it's wrong to manufacture or trade in weapons, since violence goes against Christian teachings. Islam forbids alcohol, (it's harmful and can distract a Muslim from Allah) so Muslims consider it wrong to make or sell alcohol.

Religious people are also likely to disapprove of businesses that work with oppressive regimes or exploit cheap labour in poor countries.

ENVIRONMENTALLY DAMAGING OCCUPATIONS:
Christianity, Judaism and Islam all teach that we have a responsibility to care for the environment. So occupations that are directly damaging (e.g. unsustainable tree felling) or potentially damaging (e.g. genetically modifying crops) to the environment tend to be considered immoral.

Also, anything that's harmful to animals, for example animal experimentation or organising blood sports (e.g. bullfighting) is likely to be seen as wrong (see p.14).

SEX-BASED OCCUPATIONS:
All three religions stress the importance of sexual modesty, so making money from sex is forbidden. That rules out obvious things like prostitution, running a brothel and making or selling pornography.

Most religious people would also consider it immoral to make or sell sex-based merchandise (e.g. erotic clothing, 'sex toys', etc.) or to use sexually-suggestive imagery.

There are some occupations that are only frowned on by certain religions. For example, Roman Catholics believe that in vitro fertilisation is completely immoral (see page 11), so they strongly disapprove of doctors and nurses involved in it.

Well — I say, steady on...

Occupations like teaching, social work and nursing are often considered particularly moral. Religious people are also likely to be drawn to businesses with a good human rights record, that trade fairly.

Ethics 1.3 — Religion, Poverty and Wealth

Practice Questions

Wealth tends to be a bit of a dilemma for religious people — all three religions teach that it's important to help those who are less well off than you, but does that mean you should give <u>everything</u> away? What about your duty to provide a secure and comfortable home for your own family? It's tricky.

There's nothing for it but to learn all the teachings, then have a go at these practice questions. See how many you can do — then go back through the section and work out answers for those you struggled with. Then do them again, and again, till you can get through the whole lot. Well... go on then...

1) What is:
   a) wealth?
   b) poverty?
   c) famine?
   d) gambling?
   e) usury?
   f) Tzedakah? (Judaism)
   g) Gemilut Hasadim? (Judaism)
   h) Zakah? (Islam)
   i) Sadaqah? (Islam)

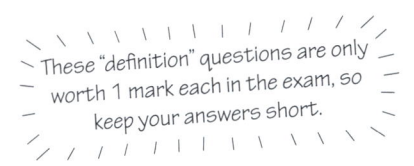

   These "definition" questions are only worth 1 mark each in the exam, so keep your answers short.

2) a) State two Christian/Jewish/Muslim teachings about wealth.
   b) Explain what is meant by charity.
   c) What is meant by a moral or immoral occupation?

   Don't write an essay for these questions. They're worth 2 marks, so make sure you get two facts down for each of them.

3) a) Describe some of the common causes of hunger/famine.
   b) Describe Christian/Jewish/Muslim teachings about charging interest.
   c) Describe Christian/Jewish/Muslim teachings on gambling.
   d) What sorts of occupation might a Christian/Jew/Muslim consider to be immoral?

   These questions are worth up to 3 marks, so you need to give a bit more detail.

4) a) Explain how poverty, hunger and disease are often related to each other.
   b) Describe how a Christian/Jewish/Muslim organisation responds to the needs of the poor, the starving and the sick.
   c) Explain why Christians/Jews/Muslims believe it's important to give money to charity.
   d) Explain why Christians/Jews/Muslims believe it's important to care for other people.

   In these questions, you'll be marked on the quality of your English as well as the content of your answer — so watch your grammar and technical terms. Each one's worth 6 marks in the exam.

5) Read the following statements:
   a) "The poverty of some is caused by the greed of others."
   b) "Religious people shouldn't be wealthy."
   c) "How you spend your money is up to the individual."
   d) "Showing compassion to people is more important than giving money to charity."
   e) "It doesn't matter how you earn your money."

   Discuss each statement. You should include different, supported points of view and a personal viewpoint. You must refer to a religion in your answer.

   These questions are worth 12 marks each, with possible extra marks for spelling, punctuation and grammar. You <u>must</u> refer to the religion you're studying (Christianity, Judaism or Islam) but you can stick in other stuff as well.

Ethics 1.3 — Religion, Poverty and Wealth

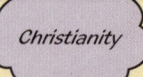

Attitudes to War: Christianity

Although Christianity is generally 'anti-war', many denominations accept that a war can be 'just' (i.e. justified). Individuals may not agree with this, however. They may be against war under any circumstances.

There are Five Conditions for Declaring a Just War

1) Christianity teaches that peace is the ultimate goal for all human beings.
2) Peace doesn't just mean a lack of war — it's more positive than that. Peace is a total freedom from distress and disturbance that Christians believe can be brought about by 'good will' and faith.
3) Although Christians recognise that war goes against the teachings of Jesus, most Christian denominations accept that there can be such a thing as a 'just war'. According to the current Catechism of the Roman Catholic Church (a sort of religious handbook), a just war should satisfy these conditions:

PROPER AUTHORITY A war must be declared by a proper authority, e.g. an elected government, a president or a monarch. *(This isn't always listed as a separate point.)*

JUST CAUSE A war must be defensive, preventing damage that would be "lasting, grave and certain" (Catechism of the Catholic Church: para 2309). This doesn't necessarily mean self-defence — defending a friendly nation or innocent people is also seen as 'just'. In some versions of 'just war' theory (but not in the Catechism) there's a separate condition of right intention. Even if there is a just cause, that cause mustn't be used as an excuse to achieve an unjust goal — e.g. to punish an enemy or gain land.

LAST RESORT All other ways of resolving the conflict must have been tried first.

ACHIEVABLE AIM A war must have a reasonable chance of success. Fighting a war you have no chance of winning is considered a waste of lives.

PROPORTIONALITY Any harm caused by fighting the war mustn't be as bad as the harm it's trying to prevent. For example, using weapons of mass destruction (nuclear, biological and chemical weapons) would nearly always violate this condition.

As well as all that, there are conditions for fighting a war justly. These are:

Discrimination: war should discriminate between combatants and civilians — it's not seen as 'just' to deliberately target civilians.

Proportionality: the military advantage gained by an attack must outweigh any harm caused to civilians.

This is different from the 'proportionality' used to justify the war. This is about individual attacks.

A 'Holy War' is one where people believe that God is 'on their side' — e.g. in the 11th, 12th and 13th centuries, Christians went on crusades to 'free' the Christian holy places in Palestine.

Pacifists are Opposed to All Violence

1) A pacifist is someone who has strongly held beliefs that war and physical violence are wrong under any circumstances. Pacifists believe that all disputes should be settled peacefully.
2) Some Christians believe that all violence goes against Jesus's teachings to love your enemy and 'turn the other cheek' (Matthew 5:38-48).
3) There were pacifists in Britain who refused to fight in the world wars. These 'conscientious objectors' went to prison — they were prisoners of conscience. They suffered humiliation in prison, and after they'd been released.

> "Put your sword back in its place... for all who draw the sword will die by the sword."
> Matthew 26:52

The Religious Society of Friends (the Quakers) is a Christian denomination that's opposed to war under all circumstances.

Just war, just cause — just learn it pal...

In the age of weapons of mass destruction, Pope Benedict XVI has questioned whether a 'just war' is possible any more. With these weapons, it's impossible to discriminate between fighters and civilians.

Attitudes to War: Judaism

Peace is the priority for Jews too. But they don't rule out violence or war.

The Jewish View — Obligatory and Optional Wars

1) The universal greeting amongst Jews is 'shalom' (peace) — this is the ideal. War is hated, but there's a belief that war is sometimes necessary to bring about peace.
2) War is divided into two categories — obligatory war and optional war.
3) An obligatory war (milchemet mitzvah) might be:
   i) a war fought in self-defence, or a pre-emptive strike in order to avoid being attacked.
   ii) a war to help neighbouring countries — so that your own country is not invaded.
   iii) a war commanded by G-d.
4) An optional war (milchemet reshut) should only take place when all attempts to secure peace have failed.
5) No war should be fought to colonise land or take revenge. This is forbidden.
6) Targeting only combatants, and not civilians, is important in war. This proverb illustrates the Jewish belief that wars should be fought humanely.

> "If your enemy is hungry, give him food to eat; if he is thirsty, give him water to drink."
> Proverbs 25:21

Jews are still Fighting for their Homeland

Zionism (after Zion, one of the hills on which the holy city of Jerusalem was built), is the belief that the Jews should have a homeland of their own — the land that G-d gave them.

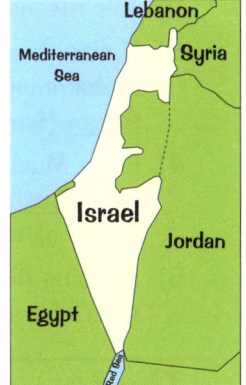

> The Jews lost their homeland in the 6th century BCE, when much of the population of Judah was taken into exile in Babylon (although many returned in the 5th century BCE). Later, the Jews suffered conquest by the Greeks, and then by the Romans. After a Jewish rebellion in 70 CE, the Romans destroyed Jerusalem. For many centuries most Jews had to live abroad — this is known as the Jewish diaspora. The State of Israel was established in 1948.

1) For many Jews the establishment of the State of Israel heralded the fulfilment of the Zionist dream. And some Jews believe that protecting their homeland justifies violence.
2) There was violent opposition to the Jewish settlement in Israel — because it displaced the Palestinians who'd been living there. This conflict is still going on today.
3) Some Jews felt that the establishment of the State of Israel was wrong. They believed it was the job of the Messiah to restore the Jews to their homeland, and G-d's people should have waited for him to come.

Jews were Victims in World War II — in the Holocaust

1) Towards the end of the 18th century, the hatred of Jews (anti-Semitism) escalated in Europe.
2) In the 1920s, Germany had huge economic problems, and the Nazi Party (a political party) blamed them on non-Aryan people (those that weren't considered 'pure Germans') living in Germany — and especially Jews.
3) Laws were passed that deprived Jews of more and more rights — and eventually, Hitler introduced a plan to wipe out the Jews completely. Huge numbers of Jews perished in gas chambers in extermination camps.

Pacifism isn't Promoted in Judaism

1) Pacifism is considered a good choice in some circumstances — when it's the only way to survive, or when using violence would be pointless. This is why Jews generally didn't respond violently to anti-Semitism.
2) But at other times, Jewish teaching demands the use of violence. According to the Talmud, if a Jewish person sees someone attempting to murder someone else, they must do whatever they can to save the person's life — even if this means killing the murderer.
3) However, using minimal force is encouraged in Judaism — so if you can prevent the murder without killing the murderer, then that's what you should do.

The Talmud is a collection of teachings that some Jews believe were given directly to Moses by G-d.

Six million people died in the Holocaust.

Six million people. Hard to comprehend.

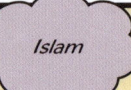

Attitudes to War: Islam

Despite the fact that there have been a number of wars between Muslims and Jews, there are many similarities in the way the two religions approach the subject of war.

The Islamic View — 'Hate Your Enemy Mildly'

Muslims believe that war is sometimes necessary, although the concept of jihad is often misunderstood. These passages sum up Muslim teaching:

> "He who fights that Allah's Word should be superior, fights in Allah's Cause."
> Prophet Muhammad (Sahih Bukhari)
>
> "Hate your enemy mildly; he may be your friend one day." Ali ibn Abi Talib

There are two kinds of jihad (or 'striving')...

The Greater Jihad

> The GREATER JIHAD is when a Muslim makes a special effort to be a 'pure' Muslim.

1) The Greater, or Internal, Jihad involves a Muslim fighting their own desires in order to please Allah.
2) This means being totally devoted to Allah, living as he commanded, and helping other people.
3) It also means following the Five Pillars of Islam — Shahadah (belief in Allah and acceptance of Muhammad as his prophet), Salah (prayer five times a day), Zakah (see p.19), Sawm (fasting during Ramadan) and Hajj (making the pilgrimage to Makkah at least once).
4) For a Muslim, the Greater Jihad may involve anything from learning the Qur'an by heart, to volunteering in the community, or perhaps becoming an imam (an imam is often a community leader as well as a spiritual leader).
5) Pleasing Allah is really important to a Muslim — if someone pleases Allah enough, they'll be sent to Paradise on Judgement Day.

The Lesser Jihad

> War is an example of a LESSER JIHAD. These wars are often thought of as 'Holy Wars'.

1) Muslims have a duty to protect themselves and their families, but wars must be fought only as a last resort.

> "And if they incline to peace, then incline to it [also]..." Qur'an 8:61

2) Military jihad has very strict rules, and is similar to the Christian idea of a 'just war':

   i) It is justified if it will bring about freedom from tyranny, restore peace, combat oppression or right injustice.
   ii) It must not be used to colonise, suppress or impose Islam on non-believers.
   iii) The sick, the elderly, women and children should not be harmed, the natural world must not be damaged, and indiscriminate killing should be avoided.
   iv) Jihad must be in the name of Allah, and according to his will. It must be declared by a religious leader.
   v) Dying in the service of Allah turns a Muslim into a martyr. True martyrs go straight to paradise as an instant reward — martyrs don't have to wait for the Day of Judgement.

3) There is no real concept of pacifism in Islam, although peace is always the goal of war.
4) Muslims believe that Allah has commanded them to live in peace with their neighbours (unless they're under attack), and show compassion towards other people.

Peace, love and harmony — seems that's what we all want...

Judaism and Islam seem to have quite a lot in common when you find out a bit more about them. That's true when it comes to war and peace as well. Neither religion believes in unwavering pacifism — the attitude of both religions is that war is sometimes necessary, though always (and inevitably) unpleasant.

Ethics 2.1 — Religion, Peace and Justice

Law and Justice

Christianity, Islam, Judaism & General

Religious beliefs about justice centre around the idea of responsibility — both in terms of answering for the things you do wrong, and of taking responsibility for the care of others.

Law and Justice are Essential to Most Societies

1) Justice is the idea of each person getting what they deserve, and of maintaining what's right. In the context of the law, that means making sure the guilty are suitably punished and the innocent are protected.
2) The courts decide whether or not someone is guilty of committing a crime, and what punishment they should face if they are guilty.
3) Different countries and religions favour different types of punishment. In general, the punishments given in scripture are fines, corporal punishment or capital punishment (see next page).

Christianity, Islam and Judaism all teach that God has commanded us to follow all laws. But some religious believers think that religious law is more important than the laws of the land.

Justice is Very Important to Christians

1) Christians believe that justice is very important, since we are all equal in the eyes of God. Christians have a duty to look after other people, and try to guide them to do what's right and repent of their sins.
2) Jesus taught that people shouldn't seek revenge when wronged — they should 'turn the other cheek'. But this doesn't mean being submissive victims — just that responses should be based on the principles of love and forgiveness. For example, if someone commits a crime, a constructive punishment could be given, to help them reform.
3) Jesus also taught that judgement belongs to God:

> "Do not judge, or you too will be judged. For in the same way you judge others, you will be judged, and with the measure you use, it will be measured to you." **Matthew 7:1-2**

Passing judgement on others is seen as hypocrisy.

> "If anyone injures his neighbour... eye for eye, tooth for tooth. As he has injured the other, so he is to be injured." **Leviticus 24:19-20**

4) However, this verse from the Old Testament puts more emphasis on the retribution aspect of punishment.

Muslims Try to Follow Shari'ah

1) Muslims have a clear and detailed religious law (Shari'ah), and this is often the basis for state law in Islamic countries. Saudi Arabia, for example, is run according to this religious law.
2) Muslims believe strongly in justice. The Qur'an teaches that Allah is just and merciful, and that Muslims should treat all people fairly and equally.
3) Muslims consider maintaining justice to be part of their role as 'khalifah' — vice-regents of Allah's creation.

Muslims believe that Allah sees all. He will know if you have committed a crime, and you will be made to answer for it on the Day of Judgement. A truly repentant sinner, however, will be forgiven.

Jewish Laws are Called Mitzvot

> "Appoint judges... and they shall judge the people fairly." **Deuteronomy 16:18**

1) Judaism teaches that Jews should obey the laws of the land that they live in, as well as following the 613 mitzvot (religious laws or commandments) in the Torah.
2) Rabbinical courts (Bet Din) exist in many countries to sort out Jewish disputes.
3) Justice is a huge part of Judaism — both in terms of what's due to G-d, and to fellow Jews. It's sometimes called a 'legalistic' religion.
4) The Torah is filled with details of laws, rewards and punishments. But, for many modern Jews, the punishments listed in the Torah are considered too extreme.

Don't pass judgement on others — that's the examiner's job...

For many religious people, justice doesn't have to come in this life, though. Christians, Muslims and Jews all believe that God is a fair judge, and that the guilty will be punished and the good rewarded in the afterlife.

Ethics 2.1 — Religion, Peace and Justice

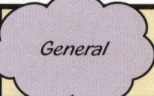

Punishment

There are several different theories about what punishment is for.

Punishment can have Various Aims

1) Punishment can take a variety of forms, including: community service, a fine, a prison sentence, corporal punishment (inflicting pain, e.g. flogging) and capital punishment (death).
2) These different punishments have different aims. For example, fines are designed as deterrents, whereas a prison sentence is primarily to protect society (although most prisons have active reform programmes too).

Deterrence: The idea that if a punishment is sufficiently bad in some way (e.g. expensive, embarrassing, restricting, painful) it will put people off committing the crime.

Protection: If a criminal is considered dangerous, this is the idea that their punishment should protect the rest of society from them, e.g. by imprisoning them.

Reform and Rehabilitation: The idea that punishment should aim to change criminals so that they won't reoffend, and prepare them for a return to a normal, useful life, e.g. by improving their education or teaching them a trade.

Retribution: Some people think of punishment as a way of taking revenge on a criminal, by making them 'pay' for what they've done.
Critics of this way of thinking argue that revenge doesn't put right the wrong — that it's better to look for a more constructive solution.

3) The majority of religious people (in modern times) believe that criminals should be treated mercifully and punishments should encourage reform and rehabilitation.

Capital Punishment Isn't Used Much Nowadays

Capital punishment is killing someone for committing a crime. It's been abolished in many places. There are arguments for and against it:

FOR CAPITAL PUNISHMENT
- The risk of death might act as a better deterrent to violent criminals than a prison sentence.
- If you execute a murderer, it's impossible for them to kill again.

AGAINST CAPITAL PUNISHMENT
- A lot of murders are committed in the heat of the moment (they're not premeditated), so many murderers won't be thinking about the consequences (so death isn't an effective deterrent).
- Execution doesn't give the offender the chance to reform.
- There have been cases where someone has been proved innocent after having been executed.

1) Many Christians are opposed to capital punishment, as it doesn't allow for reform, or show mercy. In Matthew 5:38-42, Jesus said that we should set aside "an eye for an eye", in the name of love and forgiveness. However, some Christians in the United States believe that capital punishment is a good thing. They say it protects the innocent.

2) The position of the Torah is very clear on the issue. Judaism will allow execution for murder if the case is absolutely certain (i.e. there are reliable witnesses). Most Jews are in favour of mercy, though.

> "If anyone takes the life of a human being, he must be put to death."
> **Leviticus 24:17**

The 'Howard League for Penal Reform' was set up by Christians to campaign for punishments that allow offenders to reform.

3) The Qur'an also clearly states the crimes that can be punished by death, but encourages the family of the victim to accept compensation instead.

> "...prescribed for you is legal retribution for those murdered — the free for the free, the slave for the slave, and the female for the female. But whoever overlooks from his brother anything, then there should be... payment to him with good conduct. This is an alleviation from your Lord and a mercy..." **Qur'an 2:178**

For the death penalty to apply in Islam, there must be a confession, or witnesses to the crime.

Wait, wait, he's inno... (bzzzzzz) — oops...

The Torah can be a bit extreme when it comes to punishment — have a read of Leviticus 20 and 24 (gulp!).

Social Injustice

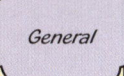

Social injustices are unfairnesses in society rather than specific cases that can be tackled by the law.

Social Injustice means Not Treating Everyone Fairly

1) 'Social injustice' can mean:
   - Groups of people being unfairly disadvantaged, so they don't get the same opportunities in society as other groups of people (i.e. being discriminated against).
   - An uneven distribution of the benefits of society (e.g. wealth).
2) The first type of social injustice includes discrimination on the grounds of race, gender, religion, social class, poverty, age or disability. (See pages 29-35 for religious teachings on discrimination and prejudice).
3) The second type of social injustice comes about when some members of society are very wealthy while others struggle to meet their basic needs — food, shelter, warmth, etc.
4) Most religious believers see it as their duty to fight social injustice (see pages 17-19 and 30-33).

Social Justice is Based on the Idea of Human Dignity

1) Most Christians, Jews and Muslims believe that all people deserve to be treated fairly and with respect, simply because they're human.
2) This is based on a belief in human dignity — the idea that all human life is valuable, regardless of religion, race, gender, age, social class, etc.
3) For Christians and Jews, the idea of human dignity is based on the teaching that God created man in his own image, i.e. humans are believed to be in some way like God.

Despite Ben's squawking about human dignity the bow remained.

"So God created man in his own image, in the image of God he created him; male and female he created them." Genesis 1:27

4) Many Christians and Jews believe that human consciousness, self-knowledge, reason and free will are examples of these 'godly' qualities, bestowed on humans, but not on any other form of life.

"And We have certainly honoured the children of Adam... and preferred them over much of what We have created, with [definite] preference." Qur'an 17:70

5) Islam teaches that human life is sacred, because Allah created Adam (the first man) with his own hands, and breathed a soul into him: "...I have proportioned him and breathed into him of My [created] soul..." (Qur'an 38:72).
6) Allah then honoured Adam by ordering all the angels and jinn (spirits) to bow down to him.

Dignity and Equality Don't Mean We're All the Same

1) Although most religious people believe that we're all equally important in the eyes of God, they don't believe that we're all created the same.
2) Christians, Jews and Muslims believe that God blesses each individual with his or her own abilities, personality, talents and ambitions.
3) So, for many religious people, social justice isn't about making sure everyone has the same stuff or does the same things. It's about making sure that nothing prevents someone from using their 'God-given' talents.
4) Many campaigns to reduce social injustice focus on wealth — since poverty can be a big stumbling block to achievement. Higher taxes for people on high incomes, scholarships for poor but gifted students and free access to healthcare and education aim to even things up a bit.

From each according to ability — to each according to need...

An extreme example of social justice is Communism, where all wealth is owned collectively. Everyone contributes to society to the best of their abilities, and everyone's needs are met, whatever they contribute.

Practice Questions

Can't we all just learn to get along? Well, no — you have to learn all the stuff in this section first. This covers some pretty big issues — war, justice, human dignity... and it's your job to pick your way through this muddle that we call twenty-first century society.

And to help you in that very task...

If you can answer all these questions without breaking a sweat, you'll be well set come exam day. If you get stuck, look back at the section and then try again. Don't give up until you can answer them <u>all</u>.

1) What is:
   a) war?
   b) pacifism?
   c) a victim?
   d) the Holocaust? (Judaism)
   e) jihad? (Islam)
   f) justice?
   g) Shari'ah? (Islam)
   h) mitzvot? (Judaism)
   i) capital punishment?

   Every question in the exam starts with defining a key term. If you don't <u>learn</u> the definitions (and they're all in the <u>glossary</u>), you're throwing away an easy mark.

2) a) What is meant by 'proportionality' in war? (Christianity)
   b) Describe Christian/Jewish/Muslim teachings about peace.
   c) State two possible aims of punishment.
   d) Give two examples of social injustice.

   These 2-mark questions just check that you know the basic facts about the religions you're studying.

3) a) Describe what Christians mean by a 'just war'. (Christianity)
   b) Describe what Jews mean by an 'obligatory war'. (Judaism)
   c) Describe what Muslims mean by a 'lesser jihad'. (Islam)
   d) Describe Christian/Jewish/Muslim teachings about obeying the law.
   e) Describe Christian/Jewish/Muslim teachings about the treatment of criminals.

   Don't get carried away with these questions. They're only worth 3 marks each, so you don't have to write an essay. Just get the facts down.

4) a) Explain Christian/Jewish/Muslim teachings about war.
   b) Explain Christian/Jewish/Muslim teachings about pacifism.
   c) Explain why Christians/Jews/Muslims believe that justice is important.
   d) Explain why some Christians/Jews/Muslims support the use of capital punishment while others do not.
   e) Explain Christian/Jewish/Muslim teachings about social injustice.

   If you're struggling with the <u>structure</u> of your answer, have a look at page 45. These are worth 6 marks each.

5) Read the following statements:
   a) "Religious people should never go to war."
   b) "People should always obey the law."
   c) "The aim of punishment should be rehabilitation." *Elizabeth Fry*
   d) "Religious people should oppose capital punishment."
   e) "Everyone should be treated the same by society."

   Discuss each statement. You should include different, supported points of view and a personal viewpoint. You must refer to a religion in your answer.

   These bad boys are worth 12 marks each. You need to learn <u>both sides</u> of the big arguments to do well — no matter how passionately you believe in your own opinion. Don't forget, you'll also be assessed on your spelling, grammar and punctuation for these questions.

Ethics 2.1 — Religion, Peace and Justice

Ethics 2.2 — Religion and Equality

Prejudice and Equality

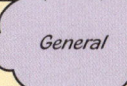
General

The world we live in is full of people from different religious, racial and cultural backgrounds. And the way each religion deals with this is important, as it can help or hinder the battle against prejudice.

Prejudice has Many Causes

It's worth being very clear about what a few words mean...

> **Equality** — being equal, and being treated equally.
> **Community** — the people living in a certain place, or a group of people with the same religious or cultural characteristics.
> **Prejudice** — judging something or someone with no good reason, or without full knowledge of a situation.
> **Discrimination** — unjust treatment, often resulting from prejudice.

1) Prejudice has many causes, and is often the product of early influences. It tends to be the result of widely held (yet inaccurate) beliefs.
2) Discrimination comes in many forms... Individuals may discriminate by being violent and abusive. Whole societies may discriminate by passing laws which prevent certain people from doing certain things.

Racism is One Form of Prejudice

It's a sad fact that some people are prejudiced against anyone from a different cultural or religious background, or simply because of the colour of their skin.

1) There have been many instances of racial discrimination in the UK in recent years — usually as a result of ignorance, misunderstanding or segregation. At times these have culminated in rioting or murder.

   Racial segregation is when people of different races do their daily activities separately — either because they're forced to, or because it's the social norm.

2) Racism is often based on stereotypes — fixed and standardised images of groups of people, which can be used to promote negative thoughts and actions.
3) The media has an important role to play. Television and newspapers can educate — or help fuel negative stereotypes (see pages 38-42).
4) More than 80% of all hate crime (crime driven by prejudice) is racially motivated. These racist crimes lead to further segregation and increased hostility within communities.

Better Community Cohesion could Reduce Racism

1) The UK is a multi-ethnic, multi-faith society (see page 34), so it can be hard for members of a community to feel they have much in common — they can lack 'community cohesion'.
2) This is particularly true of places where there are lots of people from ethnic minorities.
3) The Government is trying to promote the idea of 'Britishness' as something that goes beyond racial and cultural differences to help tie communities together.
4) The Race Relations Act (1976) is part of this. It makes it illegal to discriminate on the grounds of race, colour or nationality, or to publish anything likely to cause racial hatred.

Sex Discrimination — it's also Illegal

Most societies have historically been male dominated, and have only started to change relatively recently.

1) Up until the middle of the 20th century, it was seen as a woman's role to stay at home and take care of the family. But during World War II, women had to take on traditionally male roles, e.g. factory work, while the men were away fighting. After the war, many women didn't want things to go back to the way they'd been.
2) In 1975 the Sex Discrimination Act was passed by Parliament. This made it illegal to discriminate against people on account of their gender (sexism) — especially in the fields of employment and education.

Community cohesion — you could always try superglue...

This is difficult and emotive stuff, but like all 'Ethics' topics, it's not supposed to be easy...

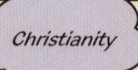

Attitudes to Equality: Christianity

For Christians, the Bible has plenty to say on the subject of equality...

The Bible has Plenty of 'Anti-Prejudice' Stories

1) The idea of "do to others what you would have them do to you" (Matthew 7:12) is a fundamental part of Christian teaching (sometimes called the 'Golden Rule').

2) Generally Christians believe that everyone was created equal by God, and so they try to avoid discrimination and promote equality. They look to the example of Jesus, who told stories about equality, and acted true to his own teaching by mixing with a variety of people himself.

3) One of the most famous stories in the New Testament is the Parable of the Good Samaritan (Luke 10:25-37) where one man comes to the aid of another simply because he is suffering.

The Parable of the Good Samaritan
A man is beaten up and left half-dead by robbers. First a priest and then a Levite (the Levites were a Jewish priestly tribe) walking down the road see him, but carry on walking. But a Samaritan (considered an enemy by the Jews) bandages the man, puts him on his donkey, takes him to an inn and sees that he is looked after.

4) But there are plenty of other biblical verses preaching equal treatment for all — these two are from the New Testament.

"...there is no Greek or Jew... barbarian, Scythian, slave or free, but Christ is all, and is in all." Colossians 3:11

"My brothers... don't show favouritism. Suppose a man comes into your meeting wearing a gold ring and fine clothes, and a poor man in shabby clothes also comes in. If you show special attention to the man wearing fine clothes... but say to the poor man... 'Sit on the floor by my feet,' have you not... become judges with evil thoughts?" James 2:1-4

Quite right too.

5) And Deuteronomy (a Book of Law in the Old Testament) includes these...

"Do not take advantage of a hired man who is poor and needy..." Deuteronomy 24:14

"Do not deprive the alien or the fatherless of justice..." Deuteronomy 24:17

By the way, 'alien' means 'foreigner' here.

Many People have Fought against Prejudice

1) Most Christians would argue that we should avoid prejudice on the basis of race, gender, religion, age, disability, colour or class. The Bible has plenty of specific teaching on these matters.

"...loose the chains of injustice and untie the cords of the yoke, to set the oppressed free... Then your light will break forth like the dawn..." Isaiah 58:6-8

2) There are many examples of individual Christians struggling against injustice. For example:
DIETRICH BONHOEFFER was a German Christian who felt that the church had a duty to speak out against the Nazis' treatment of the Jews. He later became involved in an active conspiracy against the Nazi Party and was hanged in a concentration camp.
ARCHBISHOP DESMOND TUTU and BISHOP TREVOR HUDDLESTON were active in the fight against apartheid in South Africa (see next page).
DR MARTIN LUTHER KING was a Baptist minister who dedicated his life to trying to change the way black people were treated in the USA. He organised peaceful marches, rallies and boycotts, and in 1965 blacks were given equal voting rights with whites. King was assassinated in 1968 aged only 39.

The Good Samaritan — what a nice bloke...

This is a serious issue that often makes it into the news. And it's one that you might have personal experience of — and if you do, you can use that experience to help answer your exam question. But be careful not to just rant on about yourself — you'll need to refer to the religious teachings as well.

Ethics 2.2 — Religion and Equality

Attitudes to Equality: Christianity

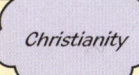

Most Christian Churches Work to Promote Racial Harmony

1) Leviticus 19:33-34 contains some basic teaching on the way that people from different races and cultural backgrounds should be treated.

   "When an alien lives with you in your land, do not mistreat him... Love him as yourself..." Leviticus 19:33-34

   This story's actually about foreigners living in Israel, but Christians argue that it also applies to the modern world.

2) There's a story about Simon Peter in Acts that's also relevant.

   Acts 10:1-35 tells a story about Simon Peter. He is told by God not to consider impure anything that God has made. So when Cornelius, a Roman soldier, sends for Peter, Peter goes willingly, even though it is against the law for Jews to associate with non-Jews. Peter says, "...God does not show favouritism but accepts men from every nation..."

3) The parable of the Good Samaritan (see previous page) is an example of Christian teaching on the treatment of people from other cultures. The Samaritans were a mixed race who suffered a great deal of discrimination at the time Jesus told the story.

4) More recently, Dr George Carey (the former Archbishop of Canterbury) spoke about the fundamental Christian belief that racism is wrong, and that everyone is created in God's image.

   "Racism has no part in the Christian Gospel... it contradicts our Lord's command... It solves no problems and creates nothing but hatred and fear." Dr George Carey

5) But although Christians generally work to improve racial harmony (people of all races living and working together peacefully), there have been occasions when this hasn't been the case...

   Not really what we were after, guys...

   The Dutch Reformed Church of South Africa (DRC) believed that God had divided mankind into different races and made white people superior. This idea became law in the system of apartheid.
   Trevor Huddleston (an English bishop working in South Africa) argued that apartheid was against God's will. For nearly 50 years, he struggled against it using non-violent methods, until apartheid eventually ended in 1994.

Sex Discrimination — Not So Clear

1) The Bible gives different messages on the subject of sex discrimination. In the New Testament, women are found among Jesus's followers and he treated them equally — remarkable for the time.

2) But this is taken from St Paul's letter to his assistant Timothy:

3) Although in Galatians 3:28 St Paul writes, "There is neither... male nor female, for you are all one in Christ Jesus."

   "I do not permit a woman to teach or to have authority over a man; she must be silent. For Adam was formed first, then Eve... it was the woman who was deceived and became a sinner. But women will be saved through childbearing..." 1 Timothy 2:12-15

Women in the Christian Church

There's evidence from the Bible that women, as well as men, taught and led congregations in the very early Christian Church, e.g. Phoebe (Romans 16:1-2), Priscilla (Acts 18:26, 1 Corinthians 16:19, Romans 16:3), Mary, Tryphena and Tryphosa (Romans 16:12).

But for much of the Church's history, women haven't been allowed to be ordained as priests. Over the last 50 years, this has started to change (see p.1)

Racism — still a big issue today, unfortunately...

In the UK, prejudice against Muslim Asians has increased in recent years. This has led to further mistrust and calls for segregation from some, and an increased desire for tolerance and integration from others.

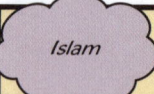

Attitudes to Equality: Islam

Islam is truly international — with followers from many countries, and many ethnic and cultural backgrounds.

Islam says People are Created Equal, but not Identical

1) Islam teaches that all people were created by Allah, and were created equal (although not the same). He intended humanity to be created with differences. But this just means that we're all individuals. Hurrah.

"And of His signs is the creation of the heavens and the earth and the diversity of your languages and your colours..." Qur'an 30:22

2) Muslims all over the world are united through the ummah — the community of Islam. The ummah consists of all Muslims, regardless of colour, nationality, tradition (i.e. Sunni or Shi'ite) and so on. This can help promote racial and social harmony, as no one is excluded or discriminated against (in theory).

Muslims are more likely to be subjected to racially motivated attacks, abuse and murder than their white neighbours in the UK.

As a result a number of peaceful pressure groups have been established — some working within Muslim communities, others working with the Government or with other faith groups.

3) Hajj (pilgrimage to Makkah) especially demonstrates equality. Those on pilgrimage all wear simple white garments, showing that everyone's equal before Allah — wealth, status and colour don't matter.

4) The fact that all Muslims should pray five times a day at set times, and face Makkah whilst doing so, also demonstrates unity and equality. Men and women often pray together at home — however, they must pray in separate groups in the mosque.

The Qur'an teaches that Men and Women are Equal

1) Men and women have an equal obligation to Allah in terms of prayer, fasting, pilgrimage and charity. And all Muslims, male and female, are obliged to seek education:

"Indeed, the Muslim men and Muslim women, the believing men and believing women, the obedient men and obedient women... the charitable men and charitable women, the fasting men and fasting women... and the men who remember Allah often and the women who do so — for them Allah has prepared forgiveness and a great reward." Qur'an 33:35

2) In the early days of Islam, there were many female religious scholars.

3) But there are also some teachings that might be interpreted as meaning men are superior, e.g.

"Men are in charge of women by [right of] what Allah has given one over the other and what they spend [for maintenance] from their wealth..." Qur'an 4:34

But these teachings are usually taken to mean that men and women just have different roles within the community or family — men are responsible for providing for the family, and women are responsible for the home (see p.1).

WOMEN AND THE MOSQUE

Women aren't encouraged to attend the mosque for prayer, but the Prophet Muhammad did permit it. If they do go to the mosque, they must pray in a separate group — behind (or otherwise out of sight of) the men.

Women are not permitted to lead the prayers of men, but they may lead other women. This is agreed by all traditional schools of Islam, both Sunni and Shi'ah.

Muslim feminist Asra Nomani is leading a campaign to end segregation in the mosque, and allow woman-led mixed-gender prayers. In 2005, Amina Wadud led a mixed-gender prayer in New York. Their actions have been condemned by Muslim scholars as not following the teachings of Islam.

Equal but not the same — don't try that one in maths...

In Islam, a woman's traditional role has been to create a halal homelife for the family (that is, a homelife that follows the teaching of the Qur'an), while the man goes out to work and makes sure the children are good Muslims. However, not all Muslims live in this traditional way — in some cultures there's more equality.

Ethics 2.2 — Religion and Equality

Attitudes to Equality: Judaism

Judaism

Like Christianity and Islam, Judaism teaches that G-d created people equal.

The Hebrew Bible Preaches Tolerance

Racism is disapproved of in Judaism. The Hebrew Bible (the Old Testament) has a lot to say on the matter.

1) The Book of Genesis suggests that all of humanity comes from the same source and is, therefore, equal before G-d.

   "Adam named his wife Eve, because she would become the mother of all the living." Genesis 3:20

2) Other messages of tolerance can be found in Deuteronomy 23:7, and Leviticus 19:33-34 (see p.31).

   "Do not abhor an Edomite, for he is your brother. Do not abhor an Egyptian, because you lived as an alien in his country." Deuteronomy 23:7

3) Deuteronomy 23 contains a discussion of who should be called 'the Lord's people'. This could be taken as meaning we should show tolerance for other nationalities. However, the same chapter does contain references to certain people or nations who should be excluded.

4) The Jewish people are sometimes called the 'chosen people'. This doesn't mean that they think they're better than anyone else — simply that G-d gave them additional responsibilities.

5) The stories of Ruth and Jonah (both in the Hebrew Bible, i.e. the Old Testament) could also be used to promote social and racial harmony.

The Story of Jonah...

Jonah was told to preach to the people of Nineveh, who had upset G-d. When he preached G-d's message, the people of Nineveh were humble and repentant, which pleased G-d, and so G-d spared the city, upsetting Jonah. But G-d said he was right to spare the city, and that Jonah was wrong to be upset. The message is,

"If G-d can love and forgive, we should be able to live with others too."

First I get thrown off the boat, then I get eaten by a big fish. This must be a Monday.

Before he got to Nineveh, Jonah was swallowed by a big fish and stayed there for 3 days.

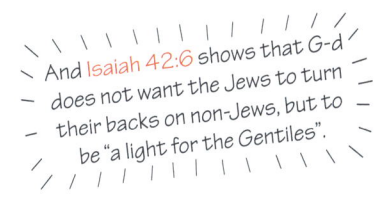

And Isaiah 42:6 shows that G-d does not want the Jews to turn their backs on non-Jews, but to be "a light for the Gentiles".

The Story of Ruth...

Naomi and her husband leave Judah because of a famine — they end up in Moab. Naomi's sons marry Moabite girls — but soon after, Naomi's husband and sons die. Ruth (one of Naomi's daughters-in-law) stays very loyal to her Israelite mother-in-law, and becomes devoted to G-d. This bloodline eventually produces King David. The message is, *"Good things happen to those who are nice to people from other lands."*

"Male and female he created them" — Genesis 1:27

1) The above passage is sometimes read as meaning that men and women are seen as equals before G-d, although different, and with different responsibilities. (G-d did create two different sexes after all, so he can't have wanted us all to be identical.)

2) Some people involved with the feminist movement (fighting for women's rights) argue that the expectation for women to become wives and mothers is unfair, and has hindered women's progress.

3) Judaism doesn't suggest that women should not be able to follow their chosen career. However, there is still a belief that motherhood is a privilege, and that women should devote some of their life to it.

4) But there are definitely differences of opinion on this. Orthodox Jews aim to uphold many of the ancient Jewish traditions, and so would be more likely to suggest that women should remain at home as mothers and wives.

5) However, Reform Jews are willing to interpret traditional teachings so that they are, perhaps, more relevant to the modern age. For this reason they're less strict when it comes to the roles of men and women (see p.1).

I don't believe the Jonah story — it all sounds a bit fishy...

Jews have suffered from a great deal of racism and persecution over the years. By far the most extreme form of social injustice was the Holocaust in World War II, when discrimination became government policy. It serves as a reminder to everyone of how much suffering can arise from racial hatred.

Ethics 2.2 — Religion and Equality

> Christianity

Attitudes to Other Religions

Christianity is a very diverse faith, with many different denominations under the Christian umbrella. But that's not to say that it's always been particularly tolerant of other religions.

The UK is a Diverse, Multi-Faith Society

1) The United Kingdom is a very diverse, multi-faith society, and religious freedom is a legal right.
2) In most major towns and cities you will find a variety of places of worship — including different churches, synagogues and mosques.
3) Children in most UK schools are taught about all major world faiths in an attempt to increase understanding and tolerance.

Although some Roman Catholic and other faith schools limit the amount of time spent looking at other religions.

4) Christianity is generally tolerant of other religions, both in the UK and globally. However, this hasn't always been the case.
5) In the past, Christians often believed they had the right to make people accept Christianity as the only true faith. Other religions were often seen as being primitive...

In the 19th century (when Britain ruled about a third of the world), Christianity was often forced upon other cultures.

In the crusades of the 11th, 12th and 13th centuries Christians attempted to reclaim the Holy Land from the Muslims. They believed that they were fighting a Holy or Just War against infidels (unbelievers) — see p.22.

Christians Believe Christianity is the Only True Faith

1) Christians generally believe that people have the right to practise any faith, although they might argue that only Christianity has the truth about God. This passage stresses the Christian belief that it is only through following the teachings of Jesus Christ that people can reach God.

"I am the way and the truth and the life. No one comes to the Father except through me." John 14:6

2) In the decree "Ad Gentes", the Roman Catholic Church makes it clear that "...the Church still has the obligation and also the sacred right to evangelise all men".
3) 'Evangelise' means spread the Christian message with the aim of converting people to the faith. Many 'evangelical preachers' or 'evangelical churches' base much of their work on this principle. Evangelical Christians consider it a priority to 'win people for Christ', because they don't believe that a person can get to Heaven in any other way.

Ecumenism is a principle within Christianity. Its aim is to create unity amongst the different Christian traditions, e.g. Roman Catholics, Anglicans, Methodists, etc.

4) There are also Christian missionaries who work all over the world spreading the message of Christianity and trying to convert people.
5) Some of these approaches may be described as exclusive — they don't particularly welcome other faiths, and may even reject them because Christianity is seen as the only way.

Pluralists say there's Room for Everyone

1) Most Christians are happy to live alongside other faiths. Organisations representing every major faith in the UK belong to the 'Inter Faith Network for the UK'.
2) The aim of this network is to promote mutual understanding and combat prejudice. This is an example of religious pluralism — the idea that every faith has as much right to exist as any other, and that there's room for everyone.

The Inter Faith Network for the UK describes itself as based "...on the principle that dialogue and cooperation can only prosper if they are rooted in respectful relationships which do not blur or undermine the distinctiveness of different religious traditions".

Pluralism — is that, like, being against more than one of something...

Christians believe they have a duty to 'spread the gospel', so that everyone is given the chance to follow Jesus. This is called the 'Great Commission'. But evangelism can cause friction in a multi-faith society.

Ethics 2.2 — Religion and Equality

Attitudes to Other Religions

Islam & Judaism

Christianity, Islam and Judaism have a great deal in common, and their approach to other religions is generally one of tolerance and mutual understanding. Over the years, though, there have been times of misunderstanding, ignorance and intolerance, which have led to discrimination and war.

Muslims Believe Islam is the Only True Faith

1) Islam teaches that people should be tolerant of each other, because Allah created all humanity from "one soul" (Qur'an 4:1) and "made you peoples and tribes that you may know one another" (Qur'an 49:13).

2) Muslims believe that Islam is the only true faith. There is, however, an acceptance that all righteous people will be favoured by Allah, as he knows all we do.

> "Indeed, those who believed and those who were Jews or Christians... those [among them] who believed in Allah and the Last Day and did righteousness — will have their reward with their Lord..." Qur'an 2:62

3) Muslims believe that men like Adam, Ibrahim (Abraham), Musa (Moses) and Isa (Jesus) were all Prophets of Allah. So the Torah and the Bible are also holy scriptures revealed by Allah (albeit edited from their original form).

4) Some Muslims use the scriptures to argue that Islam should be exclusive, and shouldn't have anything to do with other faiths.

5) Muslims are generally happy to accept converts, but they don't usually go out trying to convert people. However, some Muslims do feel that they have a mission to lead non-Muslims to Allah.

6) Many Muslims think that rejecting Islam to take another faith (apostasy) is a terrible sin against Allah.

7) Muslims in the UK often live side by side with other religious believers, and some take part in interfaith groups (see previous page).

E.g. The Centre for the Study of Islam and Christian-Muslim Relations.

Jews believe Judaism is the Only True Faith (for Jews)

1) Judaism teaches that it is the only true faith for Jews to follow, but is tolerant of other faiths.

2) Most faiths have similar moral and spiritual laws and so are tolerated by Judaism. Because of this, there's no real desire to convert people.

3) While the early Jews did accept converts to the faith, modern Orthodox Jews aren't very keen to at all. Reform Jews will accept converts after a period of study (usually about 18 months) but they don't encourage conversion either.

4) People of any religion are generally deemed to be righteous if they follow the Noahide Code — the moral laws given to Noah by G-d after the flood that prohibit idolatry, murder, theft, sexual immorality and blasphemy. And all righteous people will have a share in a world (or a new age) where humanity will be united under G-d.

...and that whole tearing the flesh from a still-living animal and eating it thing — that's right out.*
Aww... you're joking?
Baaa!!

5) In the Middle Ages, many Jews were forced to convert to Christianity. Traditionally, rejecting Judaism, and encouraging other Jews to do the same, was a sin punishable by death.

6) Islam and Judaism have very similar beliefs in one all-powerful god.

7) However, some Jews have difficulties with the Christian belief that Jesus Christ was the incarnation of G-d. And with the use of statues and icons in Roman Catholic and Orthodox Christianity, which they see as idolatry.

8) But there's still a great deal of mutual respect, and Jewish participation in interfaith groups is common. One example of an interfaith group in the UK is 'The Council of Christians and Jews'.

I know what you're thinking — this is a righteous page...

Christianity, Judaism and Islam have a lot in common — which comes as a shock to some people. But don't go getting the idea that these are the only three religions in the world. If you want to do another RS Exam after this one, there'll be plenty of other stuff to learn about. Hurrah! ... ... I said HURRAH! ... oh...

* Noahide Law No. 6 — mmm... lovely

Ethics 2.2 — Religion and Equality

Christianity, Judaism & Islam

Forgiveness and Reconciliation

Tolerance and forgiveness often need to go hand in hand.

In Christianity Love and Forgiveness go Together

1) Forgiveness means stopping being angry with someone who's done something wrong. Christianity teaches that forgiveness comes from love.
2) Christians believe that Jesus died on the cross to atone for the sins of all those who believed in him, so that God might forgive our sins.
3) Jesus taught that God is always ready to forgive us, but we must accept that forgiveness, and forgive others in turn.

"For if you forgive men when they sin against you, your heavenly Father will also forgive you. But if you do not forgive men their sins, your Father will not forgive your sins." Matthew 6:14-15

Zacchaeus (Luke 19:1-10)
A story illustrating Jesus putting forgiveness into practice... Jesus goes as a guest to the home of the hated tax collector Zacchaeus, whose life is completely changed after he decides to repent.

4) Forgiveness is closely related to repentance. Christians believe that God's forgiveness can only come when we repent of our sins (i.e. say we are sorry, and turn our backs on them).
5) If we repent, and put our faith in God, God forgives us and we are reconciled with him. Christians believe the same sort of reconciliation (coming together and making peace) is needed between people.

Forgive Your Enemies

"If someone strikes you on the right cheek, turn to him the other also." Matthew 5:39

1) Jesus taught that people shouldn't seek revenge — he said that they should instead forgive, and 'turn the other cheek'.
2) But some people think that it's wrong to keep forgiving people — that if they reoffend they shouldn't be forgiven again (although Jesus said we should forgive "not seven times, but seventy-seven times" — Matthew 18:22).
3) There are also some evils that are very hard to forgive. Should we forgive Adolf Hitler or Josef Stalin? Many Christians would say 'yes' — it is better to forgive, for the sake of the forgiver, and leave judgement in the hands of God.

Dick's 'turn the other cheek' philosophy seemed somehow inappropriate, given the circumstances.

"Anyone who hates his brother is a murderer, and you know that no murderer has eternal life in him." 1 John 3:15

Jews and Muslims have Similar Ideas about Forgiveness

Both Jews and Muslims believe that, just as God is forgiving and merciful towards them, they should forgive other people. They should also seek forgiveness and make atonement for any wrongs they've committed. The Torah and the Qur'an both encourage people to be forgiving and to seek forgiveness.

Specifically Jewish Beliefs About Forgiveness

1) The Medieval rabbi Maimonides wrote in the Mishneh Torah: "It is forbidden to be obdurate... when asked by an offender for forgiveness, one should forgive with a sincere mind and a willing spirit."
2) Jews believe that you can only be forgiven by the one you've injured, so G-d can only forgive a sin against G-d, not another person. Each year, before Yom Kippur (the Day of Atonement), Jews seek forgiveness from anyone they feel they've hurt during the year.
3) At Yom Kippur, Jews seek G-d's forgiveness for their sins against him at the start of the Jewish Year.

Specifically Muslim Beliefs About Forgiveness

1) The Qur'an allows Muslims to seek retribution for injuries, but encourages them to forgive instead: "And the retribution for an evil act is an evil one like it, but whoever pardons and makes reconciliation — his reward is [due] from Allah..." Qur'an 42:40
2) Muslims believe that injuries should be forgiven if the offender is sorry and tries to make amends.
3) There are also many Hadith describing the Prophet Muhammad's acts of forgiveness, and other Muslims try to follow his example.
4) According to the Qur'an, the only sin that Allah will not forgive is idolatry.

Learn it all — the examiner isn't as forgiving as God...

Members of all faiths believe that there can be no true reconciliation without forgiveness on both sides.

Ethics 2.2 — Religion and Equality

Practice Questions

This is all really fundamental stuff. It's about <u>tolerance</u> and <u>mutual understanding</u>. It's about the way <u>all</u> human beings should expect to be treated — regardless of race, gender or religion.
Deep.
But what it's <u>also</u> about is getting you through the 'Religion and Equality' bit of your exam. And that's where these questions come in. If there are any that you can't answer, go back and look at the relevant pages, then try again. Off you go...

1) What is:
   a) equality?
   b) prejudice?
   c) racism?
   d) sexism?
   e) evangelising? (Christianity)
   f) ecumenism? (Christianity)
   g) conversion?
   h) forgiveness?
   i) reconciliation?

   These questions get you 1 mark each — so keep your answers short and snappy.

2) a) Name two forms of discrimination.
   b) How might a Christian/Jew/Muslim respond to racism?
   c) What do Christians mean by 'missionary work'? (Christianity)
   d) What do Christians/Jews/Muslims believe about seeking forgiveness?

   These questions are worth 2 marks each. Make sure you've learnt all the basic facts for the religions you're studying.

3) a) Describe Christian/Jewish/Muslim teachings about equality.
   b) Describe Christian/Jewish/Muslim attitudes to other religions.
   c) Describe Christian/Jewish/Muslim teachings about forgiveness and reconciliation.

   These are worth 3 marks each. Don't worry too much about connecting your points for this question — just get the facts down.

4) a) Explain Christian/Jewish/Muslim teachings about racial equality.
   b) Explain Christian/Jewish/Muslim teachings on the role of women in society.
   c) Explain Christian/Jewish/Muslim attitudes to conversion.
   d) Explain how Christian/Jewish/Muslim beliefs about forgiveness and reconciliation might affect believers' lives.

   These are worth 6 marks. Make sure you write properly-structured answers for these questions and the next ones. And remember: 'explain' means you have to say <u>why</u> people believe what they do.

5) Read the following statements:
   a) "Truly religious people could never be racist."
   b) "Religion encourages discrimination against women."
   c) "A religion that teaches that it is the one true faith cannot be tolerant of other religions."
   d) "People should always forgive."

   Discuss each statement. You should include different, supported points of view and a personal viewpoint. You must refer to a religion in your answer.

   These questions are worth 12 marks — so you should be spending about as much time on these as the rest of the questions <u>put together</u>. Remember that your spelling, punctuation and grammar are assessed for these too.

Ethics 2.2 — Religion and Equality

Ethics 2.3 — Religion and the Media

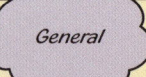

The Influence of the Media
General

The media can have a huge influence on people's beliefs and opinions.

There are Different Forms of Media

1) The term 'media' refers to any form of mass communication.
2) There are four major categories:

> **PRINT:** Anything that's printed and distributed in paper form,
> e.g. books, newspapers, magazines, comic strips, etc.
> **BROADCASTING:** Television and radio that's transmitted to lots of people.
> **INTERNET:** Mass communication via websites and emails.
> **FILM:** Cinema showings.

3) The importance of different types of media changes over time. Currently, newspapers and magazines are becoming less popular as people use the internet for their news and entertainment.
4) But digital TV and the internet don't seem to be reducing the number of books that people read. If anything, people are reading more books now than they did in the 70s.

The Media has a Big Influence on Modern Society

1) The overall influence of the media has become massive in recent years.
2) At the same time, church attendances have been falling dramatically. Many people would say that the media is now a bigger authority than the Church in the UK.
3) The media can affect people's attitudes to moral and religious issues — for better or worse...

> - Newspapers, TV news programmes and news websites carry a range of stories covering wars, terrorism, crime and politics, as well as a variety of other moral issues. It's from these sources that most people find out the 'truth'.
>
>   But some people worry about how the ideas of the people who own or write for newspapers and websites affect their content. This could include political bias or xenophobia (hatred of foreigners). The media has to strike a balance — drawing attention to problems and issues that may be of public concern, but without encouraging prejudice.
>
> - The media can educate people about different faiths — both through serious documentaries and through soaps and films (see p.41). However, misrepresentation can give a religion a 'bad name'.
>
> - Some people worry about the way the media influences people's behaviour, especially that of children. Their main concerns are about how scenes containing sex, violence, bad language and drug taking might affect the young — see page 42 for more about this.
>
>   In the UK there's a television 'watershed' at 9 p.m. After this time, programmes are aimed at adults, and it's the responsibility of parents to decide whether children watch or not. However, before this time "...all programmes... should be suitable for a general audience, including children."

4) Some people argue that the media has become too powerful. Some also reckon that the 'soundbite' nature of internet news summaries and TV news bulletins discourages people from thinking deeply about important issues.

Roll up, roll up — read all about it...

There's no doubt about it — the media has a huge power over what people believe. At its best, it can be used to educate people about a particular religious or moral issue. However, misrepresentation and bias are a serious concern for followers of all faiths. There's lots more about these issues on the next few pages.

Christianity in the Media

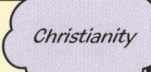

Christianity

The majority of television programming is secular (non-religious), although there are a few dedicated religious programmes to be found — and in the UK, they're most likely to be about Christianity...

You Can Find Christian Worship and Televangelism on TV

1) One of the best-known religious programmes around is the BBC's "Songs of Praise", which features Christian hymns, and focuses on a different community or theme each week.

> **SONGS OF PRAISE — SUNDAY EVENINGS, BBC 1**
> 1) Viewers share other people's experiences of God and faith. This can help show the relevance of Christianity to people's lives, and make them feel part of a larger community (although it can be hard to feel personally involved in a service when you're watching it on TV).
> 2) The programme is mainly aimed at people who are already Christian, but the themes covered are intended to give believers and non-believers alike a deeper understanding of the Christian religion.
> 3) The programme is interactive — with hymn and prayer text appearing on screen.

2) BBC Radio 4 also broadcasts religious programmes, including "Sunday Worship" on a Sunday morning. This allows Christians who can't get to church (or who prefer to worship privately) to take part in an act of worship in their own homes.
3) Evangelical Christian preachers can also be seen on digital, cable and satellite TV in the UK (e.g. GOD TV). They speak to people in their homes, delivering God's message, trying to 'win people for Christ' (convert them to Christianity) and fundraising. This is known as televangelism.
4) There are also regular Christian magazines published, including 'The Gospel Magazine' (launched in 1766 — one of the oldest magazines still in print).

Christian Religious Leaders Often Appear in the News

1) Christian leaders such as the Pope (leader of the Roman Catholic Church) and the Archbishop of Canterbury (leader of the Church of England) often appear in the media giving their opinions on all sorts of issues.
2) These issues range from whether social networking sites are harmful to young people, to what should be done about climate change.
3) Their messages are sometimes presented out of context, making them sound more controversial. This makes for exciting headlines — which sells more papers, but can give a very bad impression of Christianity.

> In 2009, the media claimed that the Pope had told people in Africa (where AIDS is really common) that using condoms is wrong. This caused an uproar. But what he really meant was that encouraging sexual responsibility and faithfulness was a better way to halt the spread of AIDS.

Christianity is Found in Other Types of Media

1) Many soaps and dramas have Christian characters. However, these characters are often stereotypes — they present a poor image of Christians, portraying them as dowdy people, with old-fashioned beliefs.
2) Many films and books also feature Christianity — more on this on page 41.
3) There are lots of websites focusing on Christian issues — and all the different versions of the Bible are on the internet in handy searchable forms.
4) Many churches display posters aimed at encouraging non-Christians to become believers and attend church.

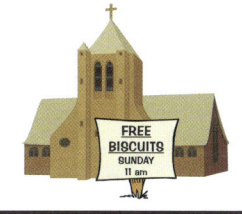

I've told you before — The Simpsons™ is NOT a religion...

Nearly 60% of people in England and Wales class themselves as Christians. The next most common religion is Islam with about 5%. So it's no wonder that most of the religious TV and radio shows are about Christianity, and that other religions rarely get a look in. They often hit the news though — as you'll see on the next page.

Ethics 2.3 — Religion and the Media

Judaism and Islam in the Media

Judaism and Islam are both involved in big conflicts — and it's usually for this reason that they get on the telly.

Israel is a Jewish Issue That's Often in the Press

1) The most common Jewish issue that appears in the British press is the Israeli-Palestinian conflict (see page 23) — although the issues are largely political rather than religious.
2) The media is often accused of imbalance when reporting this conflict. Some elements of the media are accused of being Zionist (in favour of a Jewish Israel), and of ignoring the historical context of the conflict and the suffering of the ordinary Palestinian people. Others claim that the media has a largely anti-Jewish bias, and doesn't respect Israel's right to defend itself from acts of terrorism.

But There Aren't Many Jewish Programmes

However, it's now possible to access Jewish television and radio stations on the internet.

1) Even though there are about 300,000 Jews in the UK, they're still only a very small percentage of the population. This is reflected in the lack of specifically Jewish programmes on national TV and radio — but it's still a source of frustration for many Jews.

   > In June 2008, BBC 4 broadcast an in-depth series of programmes called "Jews" that looked at the history, religious practices and beliefs of different groups of Jews in Britain today. Programmes like this may help Jews to reconnect with their faith, as well as educating the non-Jewish community.

2) The UK's Chief Rabbi, Lord Jonathan Sacks is a regular contributor to BBC Radio Four's 'Thought for the Day'. He also writes occasional articles for national newspapers — usually The Times.

Islam has Been in the Spotlight Since 9/11

1) Since the events of 9/11, Islam and its perceived links with terrorism have been all over the news. It's often portrayed by the media as a violent religion, which threatens the security of the nation. This attitude was reinforced by the London bombings in 2005, conducted by four Muslims.
2) The influence of the media has contributed to Islamophobia — hatred and fear of Islam. This has led to racially motivated attacks.

   > The Forum Against Islamophobia and Racism (FAIR) was set up in 2001 to monitor media coverage of Islam, and to work with media organisations to combat misrepresentation.

3) Programmes like Channel 4's "Qur'an" (first shown in July 2008) have tried to show a more balanced view of Islam. "Qur'an" looked at how different groups of people interpret the sacred text differently.

   > Some Other Muslim Programming:
   > - "Devotional Sounds: Islam" on the BBC's Asian Network radio station broadcasts religious music every Saturday and Sunday morning.
   > - Muslim clerics regularly contribute to Radio 4's "Thought for the Day".

4) There are lots of websites that cover Islamic issues. They're useful forums for Muslims, but they also aim to educate and convert non-Muslims. The Qur'an and Hadiths can also be found on the internet.

The Muslim Council of Britain (MCB) represents UK Muslims

1) The MCB is a large organisation of Muslim groups in the UK. It promotes peace and cooperation between Muslims and the rest of society, and provides a voice for the Muslim community in the media. The MCB's current leader, Farooq Murad, is also a trustee of the charity Muslim Aid (see p.19).
2) The previous head of the MCB, Muhammad Abdul Bari, is a well-respected community activist who holds traditional Muslim values, e.g. that people should dress modestly, and that arranged marriages have advantages. He regularly writes in the media on religion, world affairs and family issues.
3) However, there are other militant Islamic leaders, such as Omar Bakri Muhammad, who some people say have promoted violence against non-Muslims.

1.5 MILLION UK MUSLIMS BELIEVE IN PEACE — not a good headline...

The nature of the media means that the comments of religious leaders may be taken out of context to make a more sensational story. The moral of the story is take everything you read with a pinch of salt... yummy.

Ethics 2.3 — Religion and the Media

Religion in Books and Films

Christianity, Judaism & Islam

Books and films can tell religious stories, or present issues from a religious person's point of view. But sometimes they mock a religion, or present it in a negative light — and this often causes offence.

Films often have a Christian Focus...

1) The film 'The Passion of the Christ' told the story of the events surrounding the crucifixion of Jesus. Some Christians were upset by bits that contradicted the scriptures, and some felt that it was too violent.
2) Not all films focusing on Christianity aim to recount Bible stories. For example, 'Dogma' is a comedy about two fallen angels who find a loophole in Roman Catholic dogma that will let them get back into heaven. This made a joke out of Catholic beliefs, which provoked an angry response from Catholics.

The 1979 film 'Monty Python's Life of Brian' was banned by some UK councils, US states and Norway for blasphemy. The film-makers argued that it poked fun at religion, but not at Jesus.

...And Books Do Too

The Bible is the best-selling book of all time. But there are plenty of other books relating to Christianity...

1) The Bible has been produced in Manga comic style. Lots of Christians (including the former Archbishop of Canterbury, Rowan Williams) think this is great, because it's likely to capture the attention of young people. However, some people feel that it 'cheapens' the Bible, and is too simplified.
2) Books often have parallels with Christianity. C.S. Lewis's 'Chronicles of Narnia' contain many Christian ideas (e.g. Aslan's sacrifice and resurrection echo Christ's). Some Christians frown upon these parallels, while others think they're useful for telling Christian stories, and encouraging people to convert to Christianity.
3) The bestseller 'The God Delusion' by Richard Dawkins argued against the existence of God. Many religious people were angered by this, claiming that belief can't be analysed scientifically. Christians have written many books in response to Dawkin's arguments.

Judaism is Sometimes Stereotyped by the Media

1) Some feel that Jewish issues are not always dealt with fairly and that Jews are shown in a stereotypical way, e.g.:
   - passive victims in Holocaust films like 'Schindler's List'
   - neurotic intellectuals in Woody Allen films like 'Annie Hall'
   - pushy, overprotective mothers in US sitcoms like 'Will and Grace'.

'Schindler's List' was based on a true story about a German businessman who saved the lives of over a thousand Jews during the Holocaust by employing them in his factory.

2) Novels by Jewish authors bring Jewish issues to a non-Jewish audience. For example, Howard Jacobson writes comedies about the dilemmas faced by British Jews. His books don't aim to teach about Judaism, or communicate a religious message, just to entertain.
3) Some comics or graphic novels feature issues relevant to Judaism. 'Palestine' by Joe Sacco tells of the plight of Palestinians displaced by Jews. Many Jews regarded this as an eye-opening book.

The Prophet Muhammad Can't be Depicted in Films

1) The 1976 film 'Muhammad, Messenger of God' was about the Prophet's life. As Islam forbids the depiction of Muhammad and his immediate family, the story was told from the point of view of his uncle and adopted son. A few Muslims attempted to use violence to prevent the film's release.
2) Other books and films depict the lives of Muslims around the world. For example:

   'Brick Lane' is about Muslims in Britain. It was criticised for creating a negative impression of Bengali Muslims. 'A Thousand Splendid Suns' by Khaled Hosseini focuses on the oppression of Muslim women in Afghanistan.

3) Salman Rushdie's novel 'The Satanic Verses' was partly inspired by the life of Muhammad. It caused great offence to Muslims around the world, culminating in a riot in Pakistan, and Iran's Supreme Leader (Ayatollah Khomeini) urging Muslims to kill Rushdie and his publishers.
4) Comics can also be used to teach Islamic values — e.g. 'QKids' aims to attract young Muslims away from the TV and expose them to Islamic values. But comics have also been used by non-Muslims to ridicule Islam.

Now you can watch a DVD and claim it's for RS...

If books and films are too offensive, they'll be censored or banned. More on this on the next page...

Ethics 2.3 — Religion and the Media

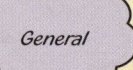

Censorship and Freedom of Speech

In the UK, people have the right to say what they believe — but not if it'll lead to too much trouble.

Freedom of Speech — You Can Say What You Like (Almost)

1) People in Europe have a legal right to freedom of speech — they can't be stopped from expressing their opinions, and they don't have to fear punishment.
2) BUT — they can't say things that will put people in danger, or that will cause disorder. There are also laws against stirring up racial and religious hatred, as well as hatred towards homosexual people.
3) Most people believe that freedom of speech is a good thing — it allows both sides of arguments to be heard, and makes 'truths' more likely to come out.
4) However, it's also argued that religious beliefs should be respected — and this often conflicts with free speech…

...and so you must kill all wearers of beige.

> In 2005, a Danish newspaper featured cartoons depicting the prophet Muhammad. These greatly offended many Muslims, leading to violent protests around the world. Supporters of the cartoons argued that they were just exercising their freedom of speech.

> In some countries, such as Austria and Germany, there are laws against denying that the Holocaust happened. The Holocaust was such an atrocity that this is a topic that pushes freedom of speech to its limits. There's so much evidence to say that it did happen, that deniers are considered highly anti-Semitic. *See p.23*

> Many Christians felt that 'Jerry Springer — The Opera' was blasphemous and some tried to prosecute the BBC, who were responsible for it being screened. The prosecution failed, which was regarded by many as an important victory for free speech.

Censorship is When Free Speech is Suppressed

1) Media items are sometimes censored (they have certain material removed).
2) This can happen if they contain material that's thought to be obscene (e.g. sexually explicit), or excessively violent, or if they cover subjects that society considers unacceptable.
3) Religious groups might also try to suppress material that they feel puts a 'wrong' message across.

> Some Christians objected strongly to the Harry Potter books and tried to get them banned from school libraries. They were worried that the books would make children interested in the occult.

> In some Islamic countries, such as Iran, most types of media (including the internet) are checked by the authorities and banned if they're considered 'wrong'. For example, websites on womens' rights are censored.

Films May Be Censored or Banned

1) Films and computer games are officially classified — some urge 'parental guidance' (PG), while others are only deemed suitable for people over a certain age (e.g. 15 or 18).
2) They may be censored too (i.e. the makers might be told to cut bits out). Sometimes certain films are totally banned in certain countries because they're too sexually explicit, violent, or go against official policy (e.g. by promoting gay rights).
3) Many people, both religious and non-religious, object to sex and violence being explicitly portrayed — they feel that this might promote promiscuous behaviour as 'the norm', and glamorise violence.
4) Some people argue that most people know that what they watch in films isn't real, and so they are unlikely to copy it.

> **Reflection or Cause...**
> Some people think that the sex, drugs and violence that we see on TV just reflect what already happens in society. But others say that showing these things has a direct influence on society, and may make immoral behaviour more likely.

You're entitled to your opinion — but mine's right...

For some religious people, their religion is such a big part of their identity that they see any criticism of it as a personal insult. But does protecting them hinder other people's right to free speech? It's a complex issue...

Practice Questions

That's it — that's the end of the book. Well, almost. There's still the little matter of these revision questions. They're exactly the sort of thing you're going to be asked in your exam. So try them, and see how you do. Then if you get any wrong, revise the stuff that's causing you problems and have another go. And keep doing it until none of it causes you any problems at all.
Well, what are you waiting for... stop dawdling and get on with it.

1) What is:
   a) media?
   b) Islamophobia? (Islam)
   c) freedom of speech?
   d) censorship?

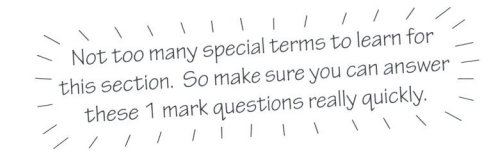

   Not too many special terms to learn for this section. So make sure you can answer these 1 mark questions really quickly.

2) a) What different forms of media are there?
   b) How might the media influence people?
   c) Why might a news report not tell a story fairly?
   d) Give two purposes for which Christians/Jews/Muslims use media.
   e) Give two reasons why printed material might be censored.

   These questions are worth 2 marks each. You need to know about the different types of media, and how religions use them, as well as their related problems.

3) a) How is Christianity/Judaism/Islam portrayed in the media?
   b) How are Christian/Jewish/Muslim leaders portrayed in the media?
   c) Why might a religious person object to how a religious character is portrayed in a television drama?

   These are worth 3 marks each, so make sure you get enough points in.

4) a) Explain Christian/Jewish/Muslim attitudes towards portrayals of sex and violence in the media.
   b) Explain Christian/Jewish/Muslim attitudes towards films focusing on religious messages.
   c) Explain Christian/Jewish/Muslim attitudes towards books and comics focusing on religious messages.

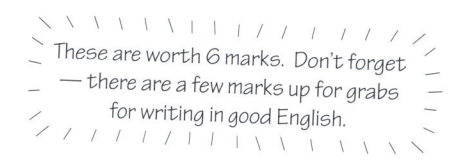

   These are worth 6 marks. Don't forget — there are a few marks up for grabs for writing in good English.

5) Read the following statements:
   a) "People should have the right to complete freedom of speech."
   b) "Films should be banned if they mock religions."
   c) "Violent films should be banned."
   d) "Films and books focusing on religion should not be allowed."
   Discuss each statement. You should include different, supported points of view and a personal viewpoint. You must refer to a religion in your answer.

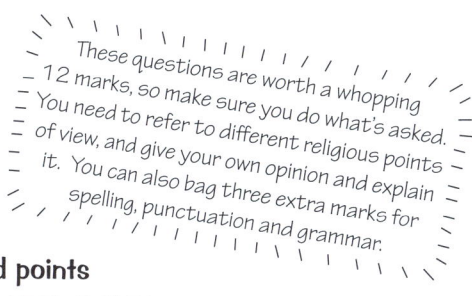

   These questions are worth a whopping 12 marks, so make sure you do what's asked. You need to refer to different religious points of view, and give your own opinion and explain it. You can also bag three extra marks for spelling, punctuation and grammar.

Ethics 2.3 — Religion and the Media

Do Well in Your Exam

You've learnt all the facts — now it's time to get those grades.

You'll have a 1-Hour Exam on Each Unit

1) For the Ethics 1 exam you'll have a choice of questions covering Religion and Human Relationships, Religion and Medical Ethics, and Religion, Poverty and Wealth.
2) For the Ethics 2 exam you'll have a choice of questions on Religion, Peace and Justice, Religion and Equality and Religion and the Media.
3) For each exam you'll have to answer two questions — you'll also have the choice of which religion to focus on for each question. You have to pick your questions from different topics — you can't just answer the same questions for different religions.
4) Each question is split up into five parts. You have to answer all the parts of the questions you pick.

You get Marks for What you Know and How you Express it

In GCSE Religious Studies there are two Assessment Objectives — these are the skills you'll need to show to get marks in the exams. You get half your marks for each.

1) The first is describing and explaining what you know.
2) The second is using arguments and evidence to explain and evaluate what you and others think.

For some of the longer questions, you'll also be assessed on your spelling, punctuation and grammar (SPaG). SPaG is worth three extra marks (see next page), so check your work carefully for errors.

There's an Easy Mark for Knowing What Things Mean

Part (a) of each question asks you to define what an important term means. These questions are only worth 1 mark, so keep your answer short and to the point — but make sure you define the term properly.

> a) What is divorce?   (1 mark)

> The formal ending of a marriage.

Learn the terms in the glossary.

You need to Know the Basics

Part (b) is worth 2 marks, which you'll get for making a couple of short points.

> b) Describe Jewish attitudes to euthanasia.   (2 marks)

> Judaism is generally against euthanasia — only G-d is supposed to decide when life ends. But in cases where someone is on life-support without any chance of improvement it may be acceptable to remove the support.

You don't need to go into depth for these questions — just a couple of details.

The question may not specifically ask for two points, but there are two marks, so try to get two facts down.

Part (c) Asks For a Bit More Detail

Part (c) is worth 3 marks — it might ask about the practices or teachings of a religion.

> c) What does Islam teach about charity?   (3 marks)

> Muslims are expected to help those in need. Zakah is one of the Five Pillars of Islam, which states that all Muslims should give a percentage of their yearly savings to the poor, regardless of how wealthy they are. Muslims believe that all possessions in the end belong to Allah, and so should be used for the benefit of everyone.

All the religions think it's important to help the poor. Make sure you write about the teachings that are specific to your chosen religion.

Do Well in Your Exam

General

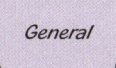

For questions (d) and (e) you're still marked first and foremost on your understanding and the facts you know. But, you'll get a better mark if you use good grammar, spelling and punctuation.

Think about the points you're going to cover before you start writing — this will give you the chance to organise them.

You'll have to Explain...

d) Explain the Christian concept of a just war. (6 marks)

> Christians have developed the concept of a 'just war' to help them decide when it is acceptable for a Christian nation to get involved in a war.
>
> According to the Catechism of the Roman Catholic Church, there are five conditions that need to be satisfied for a war to be just. The war must be declared by a proper authority (i.e. a legitimate government). There must be a just cause, e.g. it must prevent severe damage. Fighting must be a last resort. The war must have an achievable aim, with a real chance of success. There must be proportionality — any harm caused by fighting the war must be less than the harm that the war is aiming to prevent or undo.

Try to use relevant specialist vocabulary in your answers.

Don't forget to explain and develop your points.

...and you'll have to Discuss

1) Half the marks for each question come from part (e), where you'll be given a statement to discuss. To get all the marks you have to refer to the specified religion as well as including your own opinion.
2) Both your part (e) answers will be assessed for spelling, punctuation and grammar (SPaG), but you'll only get the extra marks for the one where your SPaG score was higher (up to a maximum of 3 marks).

e) "Humans have the right to use animals in medical research."
Discuss this statement. You should include different, supported points of view and a personal viewpoint. You must refer to Christianity in your answer. (12 marks)
✎ *Spelling, punctuation and grammar* (3 marks)

> Many Christians believe that animals don't have souls, and that God created us as superior to them. Some Christians also believe that animals were put on Earth for our use. In Genesis, God says "rule over the fish of the sea and the birds of the air and over every living creature that moves on the ground".
>
> However, Christianity teaches that we should treat animals kindly and not cause them unnecessary suffering. Some Christians believe that animals should only be experimented on in order to develop life-saving medicines, and not just to increase our scientific knowledge. Some Christians think that animal experimentation is wrong because they think it is unhelpful — animals often respond to treatments in a different way from humans.
>
> I believe that humans should use animals for medical research, because discoveries may be made that save thousands of lives in the future. However, the animals should not be caused pain unless it is absolutely necessary, and should be kept in suitable surroundings, e.g. not in tiny cages.

Discuss different perspectives.

Make a very clear reference to the specific religion.

It won't hurt if you remember a little bit of scripture.

To get the best marks you must include your own personal response.

Try to look at both sides of the argument.

Thou shalt write clearly...

As much as you may know every little fact that pops up in this book, a large chunk of how well you do in the exams will come down to, well... how good you are at exams. Make sure you spend enough time reading through these pages, and enough time practising doing exam-style questions under timed conditions. It'll all pay off in the end.

Do Well in Your Exam

Spelling, Punctuation and Grammar

General

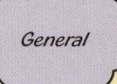

You get marks in your exams for having good SPaG (spelling, punctuation and grammar). This stuff might not be particularly thrilling but if you can get it right, it's easy marks. This page is about checking your work...

Remember to Check what you've Written

1) Leave 5 minutes at the end of the exam to check your work.
2) 5 minutes isn't long, so there won't be time to check everything thoroughly. Look for the most obvious spelling, punctuation and grammar mistakes.
3) Start by checking your answer to one of the questions which award SPaG marks (see p.44-45 for more on this). Then check your answer to the other SPaG question. Only check the rest of your answers if you've got time.

Check for common Spelling Mistakes

Check for missing words as well as misspelt words.

When you're writing under pressure, it's easy to let spelling mistakes creep in, but there are a few things you can watch out for:

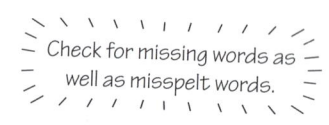

1) Look out for words which sound the same but mean different things and are spelt differently. Make sure you've used the correct one. For example, 'their', 'they're' and 'there':

> The Bible talks about wives submitting to their husbands.

> Muslims believe Allah has commanded them to live in peace unless they're under attack.

> Abortion is allowed if there is a threat to the mother's health.

2) Don't use text speak, and always write words out in full. For example, use 'and' instead of '&' or '+'. Don't use 'etc.' when you could give more examples or a better explanation.
3) Make sure you've used the appropriate technical terms (like 'euthanasia', 'sacrament' or 'Shari'ah'). If they're spelt correctly it'll really impress the examiner.

Make sure your Grammar and Punctuation are Correct

1) Check you've used capital letters, full stops and question marks correctly (see p.49).
2) Make sure your writing isn't too chatty and doesn't use slang words. It should be formal.
3) Watch out for sentences where your writing switches between different tenses. You should usually stick to one tense throughout your answer (don't worry if you've used a quote that's in a different tense though).
4) Check that you've started a new paragraph every time you make a new point. It's important that your answer isn't just one long block of text (see p.49).
5) Watch out for tricksy little grammar mistakes:
   - Remember — 'it's' (with an apostrophe) is short for 'it is' or 'it has'. 'Its' (without an apostrophe) means 'belonging to it'.
   - It's always 'should have', not 'should of' (the same goes for 'could have' and 'would have' too).

If you know that you often confuse two words, like 'it's' and 'its', watch out for them when you're checking your work in the exam.

Check, check, check, goose, check, check, check...

Blimey, there's a lot of stuff to check... which is why it's really important to practise it all before the exam. That way it'll be second nature, so you'll do it all automatically and make fewer errors in the first place.

Spelling, Punctuation and Grammar

General

Making a mistake in your exam is <u>not</u> the end of the world, so don't panic if you find one.
If you just cross it out <u>neatly</u> and correct the mistake, you <u>won't</u> lose any marks at all — excellent.

Make your corrections Neatly

1) If the mistake is just <u>one word</u> or a <u>short phrase</u>, cross it out <u>neatly</u> and write the correct word <u>above</u> it.

> Some Muslims believe that abortion is acceptable. In the Qur'an
> it says that a foetus is only fully human when it ~~recieves~~ its soul.
>   *receives*

2) If you've <u>forgotten</u> to start a <u>new paragraph</u>, use a <u>double strike</u>
   (like this '//') to show where the new paragraph should <u>begin</u>:

> The Third Pillar of Islam commands that Muslims give 2.5% of their yearly savings to charity. The money is collected and distributed by the mosque. **//** Christians feel it is their duty to be charitable. This doesn't always mean donating money, but could mean giving time (e.g. by visiting the sick) or effort (e.g. helping on a volunteer building project).

See p.49 for more on paragraphs.

If only someone had told Graham about the double strike.

Use an Asterisk to add Extra Information

1) If you've <u>missed something out</u>, think about whether you have space to write the missing bit <u>above</u>
   the line you've already written. If you <u>can</u>, use a ' ^ ' to show <u>exactly where</u> it should go.

> Jews greet each other by saying 'shalom', which means 'peace'. Generally, they
> believe that war ^ bad thing, but may be necessary in some circumstances, for
>   *is a*
> example in self defence, to help neighbouring countries, or if all other attempts
> for peace have failed. They believe war should never be fought for revenge.

2) If the bit you've missed out <u>won't</u> fit above the line, use an <u>asterisk</u> (like this '*') to show the examiner
   <u>where</u> the missing bit should go.
3) Write the <u>missing words</u> at the <u>end</u> of your answer with another asterisk next to them.

> Christianity teaches that animals should be treated kindly.* Some Christians
> believe that animal testing is wrong because they think it is unhelpful.
>
>   * and shouldn't be made to suffer unnecessarily.

Cross Out anything you Don't want to be Marked

1) If you've written something that you <u>don't</u> want the examiner to mark, <u>cross it out neatly</u>.
2) Cross out any <u>notes</u>. If you don't <u>finish</u> your answer <u>in time</u>, don't cross out your <u>plan</u> —
   the examiner might look at it to see what you were <u>going to write</u>.
3) Don't <u>scribble things out</u> without thinking — it'll make your answers look <u>messy</u>.

When making corrections, neatness is the name of the game

Examiners love it if your answer is neat and tidy — it makes it super easy for them to read. This means they can spend more time giving you lots of marks for the great stuff you've written. So neatness is win-win.

Spelling, Punctuation and Grammar

General

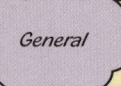

Some words are darn tricky to spell. The only way to be sure you'll get them right is to learn them off by heart. This page has some of the most common ones you'll need to know for your RS exams.

Learn these Useful Words

The underlined words are useful in a lot of answers, so you need to know how to spell them.

- There are complicated arguments for and against abortion.
- Suicide is when someone takes their own life, usually because they are depressed.
- There are definite differences in opinion between Orthodox Jews and Reform Jews.
- Christians believe it is their duty to spread the gospel.
- Not all religious believers agree about whether divorce should be allowed.
- The Jewish scriptures are basically the same as the Christian Old Testament.
- In a mosque, men and women pray separately.

Spell Technical Words Correctly

There are a lot of technical words in RS. You need to be able to spell them correctly. Learn these examples to start you off. The coloured letters are the tricky bits to watch out for.

conscience	euthanasia	celibacy	sacrament
immoral	adultery	promiscuity	reconciliation
pacifism	contraception	famine	discrimination
resurrection	justice	forgiveness	censorship
sanctity of life	procreation	prejudice	suicide

Make sure you know the specific technical words for your topics. For example, if you're studying the Islamic view on marriage, you would need to know words like 'mahr' (a dowry) and 'nikah' (the Muslim marriage contract). You can find the definitions of technical terms in the glossary on p.50-51.

You might think revision is immoral — you'd be wrong...

You could always try to make up rhymes to remember how to spell key words. For example, for 'conscience' you could have 'Mrs C, Mrs O, Mrs N S C, Mrs I, Mrs E, Mrs N C E'. Hmm, well it's a work in progress...

Spelling, Punctuation and Grammar

General

This page is full of tips for good punctuation and grammar to help you avoid making any silly mistakes, hurrah!

You need to Punctuate Properly...

1) Always use a capital letter at the start of a sentence. Use capital letters for names of particular people, places and things. For example:

   Many Jews live in Israel, where the official language is Hebrew.

   - All sentences start with capital letters.
   - The name of a group of religious believers.
   - A country.
   - The name of a language.

2) Full stops go at the end of sentences, e.g. 'Muslims worship Allah.'
   Question marks go at the end of questions, e.g. 'What is divorce?'

3) Use commas when you use more than one adjective to describe something, or to separate items in a list:

   In a diverse, multi-faith city you are likely to find a variety of places of worship, including mosques, churches, synagogues and Hindu temples.

4) Commas can also join two points into one sentence with a joining word (such as 'and', 'or', 'so' or 'but'):

   Different Jewish communities celebrate marriage in different ways, but there are some common features.

   Muslims feel that it's the right of both husband and wife to try for children, so both partners must agree to any contraception.

5) Commas can also be used to separate extra information in a sentence:

   The Jewish marriage ceremony takes place beneath a wedding canopy, a piece of cloth supported by four poles, called a chuppah.

   Mother Theresa founded the Order of the Missionaries of Charity, whose nuns now work worldwide.

   When you use commas like this, the sentence should still make sense when the extra bit is taken out.

...and use Grammar Correctly

1) Don't change tenses in your writing by mistake:

   Some schools of Islam allow abortion before 120 days if there is a good reason.

   This sentence is correct because the verbs are both in the present tense. Writing 'was' instead of 'is' would be wrong.

2) Don't use double negatives. You should only use a negative once in a sentence:

   Some Muslims argue that Islam should be exclusive and should not have anything to do with other faiths.

   Don't put 'nothing' here.

3) Write your longer answers in paragraphs. A paragraph is a group of sentences which talk about the same thing or follow on from each other. You need to start a new paragraph when you start making a new point. You show a new paragraph by starting a new line and leaving a gap (an indent) before you start writing:

   This gap shows a new paragraph.

   Jews believe that Judaism is the only true faith, but they don't try to convert non-Jews. Many faiths have similar moral and spiritual laws, so Jews are tolerant of them.
      In many ways, the beliefs of Jews, Christians and Muslims are very similar. They have similar principles and ideas about the way that believers should live their lives...

   When you plan long answers, remember that you should write a new paragraph for each of your main points.

Phew, now you're fully SPaG-ed and ready to go...

Having good SPaG is a great way to get marks in the exam, and having bad SPaG is a great way to lose marks. Which is why it's dead important to learn all the stuff on this page (and all the other pages too).

Ethics 1 Glossary

The purple definitions are only for those studying Christianity. The blue ones are for Judaism only.
The green ones are for Islam only. The rest are for everyone.

abortion	Removing a foetus from the womb before it is able to survive, ending the pregnancy.
adultery	A married person having sex with someone who isn't their husband or wife.
artificial insemination	Injecting sperm (either the husband's or a donor's) directly into a woman's womb.
celibacy	Never getting married or having sex.
civil partnership	The joining of a same-sex couple with the same rights and responsibilities as in a civil marriage.
cloning	Creating children who are genetically identical to one parent.
cohabitation	Living together in a sexual relationship without being married.
contraception	Anything that aims to prevent a woman becoming pregnant.
divorce	Formally ending a marriage.
egg donation	Using an egg from a different woman to help a couple with fertility problems to conceive.
euthanasia	Ending someone's life to relieve their suffering, especially from an incurable, painful illness.
famine	Widespread hunger caused by an overall lack of food in a region.
gambling	Playing games of chance for money.
Gemilut Hasadim	Kind and compassionate actions towards those in need.
hospice	A place where terminally ill people are cared for.
immoral	Wrong. Not acceptable according to religious teachings.
infertility	Not being able to have children.
in vitro fertilisation	An infertility treatment in which eggs and sperm are mixed in a test tube until fertilisation takes place, then a resulting embryo is transplanted into the woman's womb to develop.
ketubah	The marriage contract, which sets out a Jewish couple's rights and responsibilities.
kiddushin	Betrothal — the first part of the Jewish marriage ceremony.
marriage	The formal joining of a man and woman as husband and wife.
mahr	A dowry paid by a groom to the bride when they get married.
nikah	The Muslim marriage contract, drawn up by the families of the bride and groom.
poverty	The state of having too little wealth to live comfortably. (There are technical definitions based on income, but you don't need to know those.)
procreation	Having children.
promiscuity	Having many sexual partners.
sacrament	A ceremony by which Christians believe God acts directly on a person. Some Christians believe that marriage is a sacrament, and so can't be undone by divorce.
sanctity of life	A belief that all human life is sacred, or holy. In medical ethics, the 'sanctity of life' argument states that we don't have the right to choose when a life ends.
suicide	Deliberately ending your own life.
Sadaqah	Aid given by Muslims in addition to the compulsory Zakah, e.g. money or an act of compassion.
Tzedakah	The Jewish practice of giving 10% of your wealth to the poor.
usury	Charging high rates of interest on a loan.
wealth	Money and possessions.
Zakah	A Pillar of Islam — Muslims must donate 2.5% of their yearly savings to the poor.

Ethics 2 Glossary

The purple definitions are only for those studying Christianity. The blue ones are for Judaism only.
The green ones are for Islam only. The rest are for everyone.

capital punishment	The death penalty as punishment for a crime.
censorship	Removing material that's considered offensive from a book, film, TV programme, etc.
conversion	When someone becomes a follower of a particular faith.
discrimination	Treating different people, or groups of people, differently (unfairly).
ecumenism	A principle within Christianity that aims to create unity amongst the different Christian traditions, e.g. Roman Catholics, Anglicans, Methodists, etc.
equality	Everyone being treated equally, and considered to be just as important as everyone else.
evangelising	Spreading the Christian message with the aim of converting people to the faith.
forgiveness	Stopping being angry with someone about something they've done wrong.
freedom of speech	The right to express any opinion.
the Holocaust	The murder of millions of Jews by Nazi Germany during World War II.
human dignity	The idea that all human life is valuable and everyone has the right to be treated with respect.
Islamophobia	Fear and hatred of all Muslims.
jihad	'Striving'. The Greater Jihad is each individual's internal fight to be a good Muslim. A lesser jihad is a war fought in the name of Allah.
justice	The idea of each person getting what they deserve; also of fairness and upholding what's right.
just war	A war that's fought in a just cause, as a last resort, with a good chance of success, and with proportionality — and that's fought in a way that minimises civilian casualties.
media	Any form of mass communication, e.g. books, newspapers, magazines, TV and radio broadcasts, websites, films, etc.
missionary work	Spreading the Christian message in an area with the intent of starting up a new Christian community there.
mitzvot	Commandments listed in the Torah.
pacifism	The idea that war and physical violence are wrong under any circumstances.
prejudice	Judging something or someone with no good reason, or without full knowledge of a situation.
proportionality	In war, making sure that any harm caused by the war is less than the harm it's trying to prevent.
punishment	A penalty imposed on someone for committing a crime/offence.
racism	Discrimination against people of other races — often based on unfair stereotypes.
reconciliation	Returning to harmony and friendship after conflict.
retribution	The idea that punishment is a way of taking revenge on someone, of making them 'pay' for an injury that they've caused.
rehabilitation	A treatment for criminals that aims to change them so that they won't reoffend, and to prepare them for a return to a normal life.
sexism	Treating someone unfairly based on their gender (male or female).
Shari'ah	The Islamic law code. It's based on the Qur'an, the Hadith (sayings) and the Sunnah (lifestyle) of Muhammad, and the customs of the Muslim community.
social injustice	The unequal treatment of different groups of people, or the uneven distribution of wealth, within a society.
victim	Someone harmed by violence, or suffering any form of abuse.
war	Armed conflict between nations or groups of people.

Index

A
abortion 9-10
adultery 6, 11
agunot 5
animal experimentation 14
annulment 5
anti-Semitism 23, 42
apartheid 31
apostasy 35
arranged marriages 4
artificial insemination 11
assisted suicide 12
atonement 36

B
Bet Din 5, 25
blasphemy 42
books 38, 41

C
capital punishment 26, 35
celibacy 6
censorship 42
charity 17-19
Christian Aid 16-17
civil partnerships 2-4
cloning 11
cohabitation 6
comics 38, 41
community 29
community cohesion 29
contraception 6-7
conversion 34-35, 39-41
corporal punishment 26
crime 25-26
crusades 23, 34

D
deterrent 26
discrimination 27, 29-33
disease 16
divorce 5
double effect 12

E
ecumenism 34
egg donation 11
equality 27, 29-33
euthanasia 12-13
evangelism 34
exam 44-45

F
family life 1
famine 16
fertility treatment 11
films 38, 41
forgiveness 25, 36
freedom of speech 42

G
gambling 17-19
Gemilut Hasadim 18
Golden Rule 30
Good Samaritan 30
Greater Jihad 24

H
the Holocaust 23, 33, 41-42
holy war 23-24, 34
homosexuality 2-4, 42
hospice 12
human dignity 27
hunger 16

I
immoral occupations 17, 20
in vitro fertilisation (IVF) 11, 20
infertility 11
interest 17-19
interfaith groups 34-35
Internal Jihad 24
internet 38-40, 42
Islamic Aid 19
Islamophobia 40
Israel-Palestine war 23, 40

J
jihad 24
judgement 25
just war 23-24, 34
justice 25, 27

K
ketubah 3
khalifah 14, 25
kiddushin 3

L
law 9, 12, 25, 29
lesser jihad 24

M
mahr 4
marriage 2-6
marriage ceremonies 2-4
media 29, 38-42
medical research 14
mercy 26
milchemet mitzvah 23
milchemet reshut 23
missionary work 34
mitzvot 25
money 16-19
moral occupations 17, 20
morality 17, 20
Mother Teresa 17
Muslim Aid 16, 19
Muslim Council of Britain 40

N
newspapers 38, 40
nikah 4
Noahide laws 14, 35

O
obligatory war 23
optional war 23

P
pacifism 22-24
peace 23-24, 36
pluralism 34
polygamy 6
poverty 16, 27
prejudice 29-33, 38
prison 26
promiscuity 6
proportionality 22
punishment 25-26
pushkes 18

R
racial harmony 31-33
racism 29-33
radio 38-40
reconciliation 5, 36
reform 26
rehabilitation 26
remarriage 5
repentance 36
responsibility 25
retribution 25-26, 36
revenge 25-26, 36
riba 19

S
Sadaqah 19
sanctity of life 9
self-defence 22-24
sex discrimination 1, 29-33
sexual relationships 6
shadchan 3
shalom 23
Shari'ah law 4, 19, 25
sheva brachot 3
social injustice 27, 29
social justice 27
spelling, punctuation and grammar (SPaG) 46-49
starvation 16
stereotypes 29, 39, 41
suicide 12-13

T
talaq 5
televangelism 39
television 38-40
terminal illness 12-13
tolerance 33-36
truth 38, 42
Tzedakah 18
Tzedek 16, 18

U
ummah 32
usury 17-19

V
victims 23, 25
violence 22-23, 42

W
war 22-24
watershed 38
wealth 16, 27
women in religion 1, 31-32

Y
Yom Kippur 36

Z
Zakah 19
Zionism 23, 40